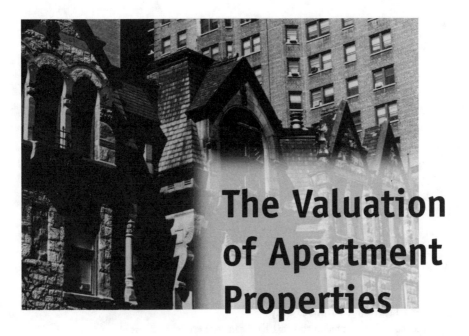

The Valuation of Apartment Properties

by

Arlen C. Mills, MAI, SRA, and
Anthony Reynolds, MAI

APPRAISAL INSTITUTE®

875 North Michigan Avenue
Chicago, Illinois 60611-1980

www.appraisalinstitute.org

Reviewers:	James H. Bulthuis, MAI, SREA
	Wayne D. Hagood, MAI
	Thomas A. Motta, MAI, SRA
	Mark R. Shonberg, MAI

Vice President, Educational Programs and Publications:	Sean Hutchinson
Director, Content Development and Quality Assurance:	Margo Wright
Manager, Book Development:	Stephanie Shea-Joyce
Development Writer:	Michael R. Milgrim, PhD
Editor:	Patricia McKibben
Graphic Designer:	Claire Krzyzewski

For Educational Purposes Only

The material presented in this text has been reviewed by members of the Appraisal Institute, but the opinions and procedures set forth by the author are not necessarily endorsed as the only methodology consistent with proper appraisal practice. While a great deal of care has been taken to provide accurate and current information, neither the Appraisal Institute nor its editors and staff assume responsibility for the accuracy of the data contained herein. Further, the general principles and conclusions presented in this text are subject to local, state, and federal laws and regulations, court cases, and any revisions of the same. This publication is sold for educational purposes with the understanding that the publisher is not engaged in rendering legal, accounting, or other professional service.

Nondiscrimination Policy

The Appraisal Institute advocates equal opportunity and nondiscrimination in the appraisal profession and conducts its activities in accordance with applicable federal, state, and local laws.

Printed in the United States of America

03   02   01   00   99   5   4   3   2   1

Library of Congress Cataloging-in-Publication Data

Mills, Arlen C.
    The valuation of apartment properties / by Arlen C. Mills, Anthony Reynolds.
        p.   cm.
    Includes bibliographical references (p.   ).
    ISBN 0-922154-54-6
    1. Apartments—Valuation.   2. Real property—Valuation.   3. Real property—Valuation—United States.   I. Reynolds, Anthony.   II. Title.
HD1387.M553   1999
333.33'8—dc21   98-43647
                                                       CIP

The Valuation of Apartment Properties

by

Arlen C. Mills, MAI, SRA, and
Anthony Reynolds, MAI

Readers of this text may be interested in these related texts available from the Appraisal Institute:

- *The Appraisal of Real Estate,* 11th edition

- *Appraising Residential Properties,* 2d edition

- *Appraising the Tough Ones: Creative Ways to Value Complex Residential Properties,*
  by Frank E. Harrison, MAI, SRA

- *Cooperative Apartment Appraisal,*
  by Eleanor Gunn, MAI, and John A. Simpson, MAI

- *The Dictionary of Real Estate Appraisal,* 3d ed.

CONTENTS

FOREWORD

Apartment properties have been highly sought-after real estate investments in the 1990s for all sorts of reasons—a growing economy, an increasing population of traditional renters, and a demographic explosion of empty nest renters. Investors have been able to take advantage of numerous opportunities to reposition properties that were hit hard by the financial woes of the late 1980s. With sale prices in all major markets skyrocketing as a result of rabid investor demand, the pressure upon the appraisal community continues to mount. As the apartment market reaches its peak, valuation professionals will need to perform increasingly rigorous analyses to justify their value conclusions and advise investors who have gotten used to prices that just seem to keep going up.

To ensure that appraisers are prepared to face the uncertainties of a volatile market, the Appraisal Institute is proud to present *The Valuation of Apartment Properties,* an up-to-date examination of the specific challenges presented by multifamily, income-producing properties. The book addresses all the nagging concerns that could cloud an appraiser's judgment, from the difficulties encountered in collecting comparable data to the problem of forecasting demographic trends.

In *The Valuation of Apartment Properties,* the authors put each of the three approaches to value under the microscope, with several examples of applied valuation techniques. Furthermore, they focus on market analysis and site and property analysis in separate chapters and include a case study illustrating the use of a 25-step worksheet to forecast market area demand and subject capture. Wrapping up the discussion—and placing the appraisal of apartment properties within the context of the general valuation process—is a useful examination of the three *R*s—reconciling, reporting, and reviewing.

Bert L. Thornton, MAI
1999 President
Appraisal Institute

CHAPTER 1

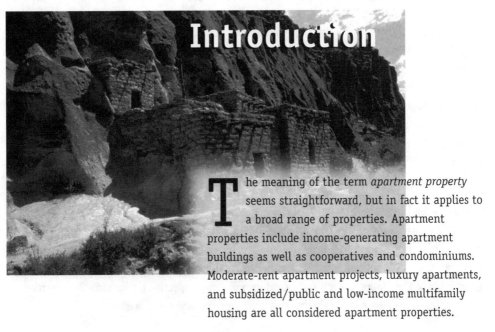

Introduction

The meaning of the term *apartment property* seems straightforward, but in fact it applies to a broad range of properties. Apartment properties include income-generating apartment buildings as well as cooperatives and condominiums. Moderate-rent apartment projects, luxury apartments, and subsidized/public and low-income multifamily housing are all considered apartment properties.

Definitions

Mainstream definitions of apartment properties vary considerably. Moreover, terms such as *apartment, apartment building,* and *apartment property* tend to overlap. *The Dictionary of Real Estate Appraisal* defines the term *apartment building* simply as "a structure containing four or more dwelling units with common areas and facilities, e.g., entrances, lobby, elevators or stairs, mechanical space, walks, and grounds."[1] The Institute of Real Estate Management (IREM) identifies *conventional apartment properties* for inclusion in its annual income and expense survey. IREM's three criteria are that the property 1) contain a minimum of 12 units, 2) lease 80% of its total rentable area as residential space, and 3) have been in operation for a full 12 months during the previous year.[2]

---

1. Appraisal Institute, *The Dictionary of Real Estate Appraisal,* 3d ed. (Chicago: 1993), 15.

2. Institute of Real Estate Management, *Income/Expense Analysis: Conventional Apartments* (Chicago: IREM, 1992), 7-8.

Individual units in the Pueblo cliff dwellings at Bandelier National Monument were owned and inherited by the matriarch of each occupying family. Photo courtesy of New Mexico Historic Preservation Division.

Apartment property has long been used interchangeably with another term, *multifamily housing*. The word *multifamily* bears the imprint of the National Housing Act of 1934 and subsequent Federal Housing Administration (FHA) legislation. While multifamily may be defined as a building intended for occupancy by more than one family, FHA-insured multifamily mortgages are typically earmarked for housing projects of eight or more units.[3] One useful definition of multifamily housing recognizes two categories of properties: buildings of two to four dwelling units (duplexes, triplexes, and quadraplexes) and buildings of five or more units. This definition further specifies that multifamily housing may be tenant-occupied, owner-occupied, or mixed.[4]

Systems of Classification

Several classification systems make it easier for real estate professionals to analyze the various types of apartment properties. These systems depend on criteria such as building height and use density, level of rent, quality of the property's attributes, and motivation for ownership or sponsorship of the property. Each system offers a useful perspective on apartment properties and supplies a framework for analyzing specific properties and their markets.

Building Height and Density

Perhaps the most widespread system breaks down apartment properties into four categories[5] based on building height[6] and density of use. These two characteristics are, in turn, determined by the local zoning and the economic feasibility of the use. This system is useful for disaggregating overall supply.

High-rise elevator apartment properties, which make up the first category, are buildings of six or more stories and represent the highest density of use. Usually, this type of property is located in or near the core of the city or a metropolitan node.

The second category, *mid-rise* apartment properties, consists of four- to seven-story buildings. They are generally equipped with limited elevator service. Mid-rise apartments represent intermediate-density developments.

Low-rise apartment properties are walk-up buildings of three stories or less, which are segmented according to the number of units they contain, i.e., 12 to 24 units and 25 to 50 units. Low-rise apartment properties are also intermediate-density developments.

---

3. E. Roger Everett and William N. Kinnard, *A Guide to Appraising Apartments* (Chicago: Society of Real Estate Appraisers, 1979), 1.

4. Jack C. Harris and Jack P. Friedman, *Barron's Real Estate Handbook* (New York: 1984), 175.

5. This classification represents a composite of two parallel systems: one is used by the Institute of Real Estate Management in its annual *Income/Expense Analysis* of conventional apartments (high-rise elevator apartments, low-rise apartment properties with 12-24 units, low-rise apartment properties with 25 or more units, and low-rise garden apartments); the other is described by E. Roger Everett and William N. Kinnard in *A Guide to Appraising Apartments,* (high-rise apartments, walk-up apartments, mid-rise apartments, and garden apartments), pp. 2-3.

6. There is no national height standard for high-rise, mid-rise, or low-rise buildings. The four categories described reflect how these terms are conventionally used and understood.

The final category, *garden* apartment properties, usually refers to complexes of two- to three-story walk-up buildings located on sizable landscaped plots.[7] Such a property may consist of 50 or more units. The site coverage by a garden apartment complex often exceeds that for the other categories. Garden apartments represent the lowest use density.

Level of Rent

A second system of categorizing apartment properties is by level of rent,[8] which defines the group that can afford the apartment units—in other words, the demand side of the market equation.[9] A breakdown of supply by rent level is especially useful in segmenting apartment markets, and it also helps in identifying competitive apartment buildings. Generally, rents are differentiated among three levels.

The first category, *high-rent* or *luxury* apartments, appeals to upper-income earners. Rents for luxury apartments are determined solely by market supply and demand. Financing for high-rent apartments comes from private equity sources and conventional loans, i.e., loans not insured by the Federal Housing Administration (FHA).

Moderate-rent apartments are sought by middle-income earners. Rent levels are generally determined by market forces, although the owners of apartment developments built by FHA-insured loans are subject to FHA rent controls. Moderate-rent apartments are built by private developers but financing may be conventional or insured.

The final category, *low-rent* apartments, includes subsidized housing, either privately or publicly owned, which is provided to low-income earners. Subsidies take the form of below-market financing or direct payment of part of the rent. Programs under the Department of Housing and Urban Development (HUD) that deal with low-income multifamily housing include Section 8 (U.S. Housing Act, 1937, and amendments, 1974), Section 23 (U.S. Housing Act, 1937), and Section 221 (d)(3) (National Housing Act, 1934). In recent years, the federal government has reduced its role as provider of low-income housing to the private sector. Some local taxing bodies offer reduced real estate assessments as a way of encouraging developers to increase the stock of low-income housing. Such dwellings are subject to rent ceilings.[10] Public housing projects are government-owned apartment units made available to low-income residents at no or nominal rent.

---

7. In the Midwest, the term *garden apartment* refers to a ground-floor or basement apartment unit with access to an adjacent courtyard or garden area.

8. The tripartite system described above is found in E. Roger Everett and William N. Kinnard, *A Guide to Appraising Apartments,* 3.

9. Tenants can be further broken down by profile. For example, singles, families, students, career people, empty nesters, retirees, and senior citizens are additional categories used to segment apartment markets. These groups are discussed in Chapter 2, "Market Analysis."

10. For an overview of the legislative initiatives that fundamentally support low-income housing, see Richard E. Poulton, "Assessment Issues in the Valuation of Subsidized Housing," *Assessment Journal* (November/December 1996): 40-43.

Qualitative Rating

A third system for classifying apartment properties is based on a qualitative rating with respect to four characteristics: rental rates and occupancy levels, age and condition, construction quality, and location.[11] Rating a property for each of the four characteristics allows the appraiser to identify the property by class: AA, A, B, C, or D. In market analysis, this system is used to rate not only the subject but also competitive properties. The rating sheds light on the comparative advantages and disadvantages of each property and helps define the supply side of the market equation. Table 1.1 illustrates the qualitative standards applied in one such system of rating properties.

Other Classification Systems

Apartment properties are also differentiated on the basis of the form of ownership or sponsorship, the motivation of the owner or sponsor, and the private or public benefits that derive from the property.[12]

The first and broadest category in this classification is *privately owned, profit-oriented developments*. These may be broken down according to investors' objectives, e.g., annual income and long-term capital gain. Smaller two- to six-unit buildings are often owned and managed by the same individuals on a "mom-and-pop" basis. Institutions or syndications, which account for much of the equity investment in larger apartment projects, include corporations (corporate pension funds), joint ventures, limited partnerships, and real estate investment trusts (REITs). Mid-sized buildings are likely to be owned by joint ventures or partnerships, whereas buildings of over 25 units are usually included among the long-term holdings of financial institutions and major corporations. The 1990s have been marked by a significant trend toward consolidation of apartment property ownership, especially on the part of public real estate companies and REITs.[13]

The securitization of real estate, which has accelerated over the past decade, complicates the investment scene. The investment performance of a real estate security does not hinge only on the equity yield from or skillful leverage arranged for a specific property. Rather, securitized investment depends on income generated by a mix of properties in a managed portfolio.

Owner-occupants of condominiums and cooperatives represent another significant category of private owner/investors. Condo and co-op owners seek a return through appreciation of the unit in which they live and intangible enjoyment of the unit's amenities.

The classification of apartment properties based on ownership or sponsorship includes two other categories: *private, nonprofit* or *limited profit developments,* which depend on

---

11. This system was proposed by Marshall F. Graham and Douglas S. Bible in their article, "Classifications for Commercial Real Estate," *The Appraisal Journal* (April 1992): 238-240.

12. This classification is based on E. Roger Everett and William N. Kinnard, *A Guide to Appraising Apartments,* 3-4.

13. Jack Goodman, "A Look at Consolidation in the Apartment Industry," *Urban Land* (November 1997): 34-37, 76.

Table 1.1 Uniform Apartment Classification

Characteristics	Class AA*	Class A	Class B	Class C	Class D
1. Rent rank	90%	80%-90%	50%-80%	20%-50%	0-20%
Occupancy level	Excellent	Very good	Average	Fair	Poor
2. Age	Less than 10 years	Less than 10 years	Less than 20 years	Less than 30 years	Above 30 years
Condition	Excellent	Very good	Average	Fair	Poor
3. Construction size	120 units or more	100 units or more	80 units or more	Any number of units	Any number of units
Construction quality	Excellent	Very good	Average	Fair	Poor
Appeal	Excellent	Very good	Average	Fair	Poor
Functional utility	Excellent	Very good	Average	Fair	Poor
HVAC	Excellent	Very good	Average	Fair	Poor
Layout	Excellent	Very good	Average	Fair	Poor
Landscaping	Excellent	Very good	Average	Fair	Poor
Parking	1 or more/br.	1 or more/br.	1 or more/br.	1 or more/unit	Not required
Amenities†	10 or more	8 or more	6 or more	Not required	Not required
4. Location					
Driving time to work and shopping	Excellent	Very good	Average	Fair	Poor
Safety and security	Excellent	Very good	Average	Fair	Poor
Neighborhood reputation and appearance	Excellent	Very good	Average	Fair	Poor

Source: Marshall F. Graham and Douglas S. Bible, "Classifications for Commercial Real Estate," *The Appraisal Journal* (April 1992): 240.

*Analysts also recognize Class AAA, which meets all the same standards of Class AA except that Class AAA has a 95% rent rank and is located in a "Tier 1 metropolitan area," i.e., the MSA population is over 1 million.

† Microwave, self-cleaning oven, dishwasher, frost-free refrigerator, ice-maker refrigerator, garbage disposal, trash compactor, ceiling fan, cable TV, woodburning fireplace, color-coordinated accent walls, wall-to-wall carpeting, other.

public programs to subsidize the rent of the tenants, lower the financing costs of the developers, or reduce the owner's property assessments, and *public housing,* which includes all developments publicly sponsored and owned by local, state, and federal governments.

Scope

This book will focus upon conventionally developed apartment complexes. Projects of fewer than eight units, housing projects for low-income tenants, and condominiums or cooperatives are referenced occasionally, but they are not discussed in depth. Smaller projects are typically valued by means of gross rent multipliers (*GRMs*) or gross income multipliers (*GIMs*), which are covered in Chapter 4, "Income Capitalization." Low-income housing can be large scale, but because of subsidies, financing may not correspond to market levels.[14] Government agencies often set the guidelines for the valuation of low-income housing. Either the sales comparison or income capitalization approach may be used. But appraisals of low-income housing complexes based on the income capitalization approach should include an allocation between the value of the subsidy, if it results in nonmarket financing or rent, and the value based on the property income.

While condo and co-op developments satisfy the functional criteria established by definitions of apartment buildings or multifamily housing, they are not apartment properties intended for rental occupancy by non-owners. In certain situations, the methods of valuation may be the same as those used for apartment buildings. For example, an income analysis is generally required when an apartment property is converted into a condominium or cooperative. Most appraisals involving condominiums or cooperatives, however, are of individual units. The valuation is related to the amenities the unit offers rather than its income-producing potential.[15] For appraisals of individual condo or co-op units, the sales comparison approach is typically used.[16]

The organization of this book mirrors the appraisal process. It describes how an appraiser goes about the market analysis and valuation of a conventional apartment property. Market analysis is the keystone of any appraisal. Here the appraiser examines the subject property in terms of demand and supply, considering factors that lead individuals and families to decide to rent or buy, to live downtown or in the suburbs, in a room or dwelling unit, or in a freestanding or attached building. Market analysis segments demand according to characteristics such as age, household size, and income. Another aspect of market analysis is the survey of supply, or an inventory of competitive properties compiled by age, ameni-

---

14. For a discussion of appraisal issues and Uniform Standards of Professional Appraisal Practice (USPAP) Advisory Opinion AO-14, Appraisals of Subsidized Housing (dealing with intangible value such as financial incentives), see Richard E. Poulton, "Assessment Issues in the Valuation of Subsidized Housing," *Assessment Journal* (November/December 1996): 43-49. For insight into the application of the three approaches to valuing subsidized housing, see Wayne Ballweg, "Subsidized Housing: An Assessor's Viewpoint," *Assessment Journal* (July/August 1997): 54-59.

15. E. Roger Everett and William N. Kinnard, *A Guide to Appraising Apartments,* 5.

16. Appraisal Institute, *Appraising Residential Properties,* 2d ed. (Chicago: 1994), 494-495.

ties, targeted market, and price. Analysis of competitive supply yields data on occupancy, rents, and expenses—information essential to developing the income capitalization approach. The relation of demand to supply provides insight into anticipated occupancy or absorption as well as the financial or economic feasibility of the apartment project.

Real estate appraisal is based upon three approaches to value. Income capitalization and sales comparison are the approaches typically used to value apartment properties. Both approaches are transaction-based and consider the entire property as an operational entity. The income capitalization and sales comparison approaches can be explained in a logical manner and are readily grasped by market participants, government administrators, jurists, and the general public. In order to conclude the present value of anticipated future benefits, the appraiser using the income capitalization approach must forecast rents and expenses beyond the effective date of the appraisal. When market conditions are unstable, forecasting becomes more tenuous. Thus, the longer the term of the forecast, the more speculative the value indication.

The sales comparison approach has limitations as well. In many jurisdictions, the details of real estate purchase transactions are not subject to public scrutiny as are other major investments. And the transactions analyzed in sales comparison are necessarily historic data.

The cost approach is an important component in any rationalization for decisions involving whether to buy, to build, or even to lease. The cost approach also provides a benchmark estimate of depreciation and insight into the highest and best use of the property. Value indications derived from cost, however, may not always reflect market conditions, i.e., the relationship between supply and demand. Proponents of the cost approach argue that in stable markets where supply and demand are in equilibrium, a value indication derived from the cost approach corresponds to the market value of the property. Balanced markets, however, are more the exception than the rule.

The inability of the cost approach to respond to market conditions is especially evident in cost calculations for nonconstruction items such as the value added by the developer. The developer's fee is expected to exceed out-of-pocket costs to the extent of the developer's contribution. In a distressed market or period of abnormally low demand for apartments, a cost approach conclusion may be flawed. The value added by developing an apartment building of perfect design and quality construction cannot be realized. Similarly, in an overcharged market, where demand outpaces supply to the extent that the value of a new building exceeds all anticipated costs, the cost approach conclusion may be unreliable.

Despite individual limitations, each of the three approaches is applicable in relevant situations. This book provides examples of the typical problems appraisers encounter in developing value estimates and the variety of benchmarks they can use to analyze apartment properties. A concluding chapter covers reconciliation, the appraisal report, and reviewing.

CHAPTER 2

Market Analysis

Purpose and Level of Market Analysis

The term *market analysis* has several meanings. In the broadest sense, it refers to the collection and study of market data required to apply the approaches to value. With existing or operating apartment properties, the principal task is gathering data from the subject and comparable properties on income, expenses, and other features (e.g., sale prices, capitalization rates, occupancy/vacancy and absorption rates). Market analysis refers to the process of determining whether marginal or residual demand exists for a given property use and, if so, the extent of that support. In this sense, the purpose of market analysis is to investigate the marketability of proposed uses for a property and thereby lay the foundation for the analysis of their feasibility and conclusion of the highest and best use of the property. This conclusion will be as specific as the market suggests. For example, market analysis may reveal whether a proposed multifamily development should be owner-occupied condominiums or renter-occupied apartment units.

Market analysis is essential to the valuation of existing and proposed properties. Existing properties normally have an operating history, i.e., a record of occupancy, rents, and expenses. The use determination for an existing property is likely to be straight-

Baroness Micaela Almonester y Pontalba commissioned the Pontalba Apartments of Jackson Square in New Orleans in 1850. Photo courtesy of Louisiana Office of Tourism.

forward. Although future occupancy and income cannot be certain, a reasonable cash flow forecast can be developed on the basis of market analysis. For a proposed property on a site that is either vacant or under another use, however, the greater uncertainty requires more in-depth study.

The appraiser is not required to develop an independent market analysis for every assignment. In some situations, the client furnishes a completed market analysis; in others, the appraiser relies directly on the work of professional market analysts. In either case, however, the appraiser must understand the steps and procedures involved.

Six-Step Process

Market analysis undertaken to investigate market support for a specific use is generally applied by means of the six-step process described below.[1]

1. ***Property Productivity Analysis*** The appraiser or analyst investigates the productive attributes of the subject property at the outset. These are features that shape the productive capabilities and potential uses of the property, i.e., its physical, legal, locational, and amenity attributes. Identifying the potential uses of the property allows the analyst to target potential users or the most likely market segment for the property.

2. ***Specification of the Market of Most Probable Property Users*** Market specification pinpoints the precise market segment to which the property will appeal by establishing the spatial dimensions and behavioral components of market demand. Accordingly, *market delineation* identifies the market area, i.e., the area in which similar properties compete with the subject property for probable tenants. The market area varies with the type and character of the apartment property (studio/efficiency versus luxury units). This process of differentiating the subject property and other directly competitive properties from the broader stock of similar properties is called *market disaggregation*. Market delineation also identifies the most likely tenants, based on consumer profiles, i.e., features such as income, age, and lifestyle. The process of differentiating the most probable tenants from the broader population is called *market segmentation*.

---

1. This procedure is explained in Stephen Fanning, Terry Grissom, and Thomas Pearson, *Market Analysis for Valuation Appraisals* (Chicago: Appraisal Institute, 1994). The first of the steps described above deals with a physically possible and legally permissible use, and the remaining steps provide essential information for determining the financial feasibility of a use. The market analysis process is a fundamental component of highest and best use analysis.

The National Council of Real Estate Investment Fiduciaries (NCREIF) has published guidelines for market area delineation, demand analysis, supply analysis, absorption analysis, vacancy analysis, and market rental rate analysis. See D. Richard Wolcott and Glenn R. Mueller, "Market Analysis in the Appraisal Process," *The Appraisal Journal* (January 1995): 27-32.

For a discussion of the theoretical and practical problems involved in performing market analyses, see the review in *The Appraisal Journal* by Anthony Reynolds (July 1995): 370-373, of *Appraisal, Market Analysis, and Public Policy in Real Estate: Essays in Honor of James A. Graaskamp,* edited by James R. Delisle and J. Sa-Aadu (Boston, Dordrecht, London: American Real Estate Society/Kluwer Academic Publishers, 1994).

3. **Demand Analysis and Forecast** Market demand, both existing and anticipated, is estimated by examining population and employment data derived from economic base analysis. The analyst evaluates variables shaping demand, such as population forecast; household size, number, and growth rate; breakdown of population by renters and owner-occupants; and breakdown of households by income, age (usually associated with income and household size), and typical percentage of household income expended on rent. With this information, the analyst estimates the size of the demographic group that corresponds to the most probable tenants in terms of space requirements, available housing alternatives, and ability to pay.

4. **Competitive Supply Analysis and Forecast** Existing and anticipated supply is inventoried according to building category, age, size, location, and rents. Anticipated supply includes properties under construction, in planning, or proposed. Multifamily housing starts and construction activity tend to vary with interest rates.

5. **Supply and Demand Study or Equilibrium Analysis** The inventory of supply and estimate of demand are compared to determine whether marginal or residual demand exists or whether such demand can be forecast at some point in the future. There may be an oversupply of apartment space in some markets. The two types of oversupply (low occupancy rates) are *technical,* when available units exceed potential tenants, and *economic,* when available space is priced beyond the purchasing power of potential tenants. Equilibrium analysis involves not only the analysis of data but also understanding of the market. Market conditions reflect the interaction of short-term real estate cycles, which are governed by the availability of credit and the level of interest rates, and long-term or secular business cycles, which depend on broad demographic and employment trends. The analyst will also study indicators of market activity, such as the terms of available financing, number of mortgages recorded, values of multifamily sales, and range between listing and acquisition prices/rentals.

6. **Capture Analysis** When the subject and competitive properties are highly comparable, the analyst may assume that each property will capture a proportionate or pro rata share of marginal demand. When this is not the case, the productive attributes of the subject property are ranked against those of competitive properties. The ranking reveals any special advantage of the subject or comparable properties and helps in forecasting the subject's probable market share under existing conditions.

Financial Feasibility Analysis A conclusion of highest and best use must be supported by this analytical process. Financial feasibility is determined on the basis of variables such as the residual land value(s), the rate(s) of return, or the capitalized value(s) of the overall property under the use(s) considered. Financial feasibility analysis also considers the risk associated with each alternative use and, for proposed properties, the specific timing of development.

Trends and Prospects

Economic and demographic circumstances indicate a positive forecast for multifamily housing in the late 1990s and beyond.[2] Demand for apartment properties is made up of the following three demographic components:

1. Young and upwardly mobile renters

2. Moderate-income, permanent renters

3. Empty nesters or seniors[3]

The aging of the baby boomer generation, that segment of the population born after the Second World War and now approaching peak wage earning capacity, will likely be the most significant component of demand over the next two decades. Numbering 75 million, the baby boomers make up 30% of the overall population. As the baby boomers become empty nesters, many will opt for more manageable, amenity-outfitted apartments over single-family housing with its associated maintenance costs.

In view of their longer life expectancies, the baby boomers will also begin to seek elderly or senior housing, a category that ranges from retirement communities to congregate facilities. Typically, elderly housing consists of apartment-style units in a community setting where common services such as housekeeping, meals, organized activities, transportation, security, and nursing care are provided. Elderly housing is expected to become a growth industry over the next two decades.

The two generations that follow the baby boomers will also exert apartment demand. Generation X, called the *baby bust generation*, includes those persons born between the early 1960s and late 1970s. Numbering 55 million, the baby busters make up a little more than one-fifth of the overall population. Generation Y, known as the *echo generation*, includes those born since 1980, when the birth rate again began to rise. It numbers 72 million. Lifestyle changes account for the smaller household size of Generations X and Y, e.g., single-person households and double-income households without children. These younger and smaller households will seek moderate- and low-income housing.

Although the strong economy has brought unemployment to a record low, wages of blue-collar workers have been fairly stagnant and for many, homes remain unaffordable. Minority and immigrant populations continue to grow. These segments of the population will also fuel demand for moderate- and low-income housing. Having abandoned many of its low-income housing programs, the federal government is encouraging the private sector to meet growing demand in this area through fiscal incentives and underwriting guarantees.

---

2. Equitable Real Estate Investment Management Inc. and Real Estate Research Corporation, *Emerging Trends in Real Estate* (Chicago: 1996), 32. The respondents surveyed in the Appraisal Institute's *Annual Economic Forecast 1997* also expressed confidence in multifamily market fundamentals, foreseeing continued marginal demand, increasing property values, and a growing number of multifamily starts. See pages 10, 18, and 35 of that publication.

3. Stephen Fanning, Thomas Pearson, and Terry Grissom, *Market Analysis for Valuation Appraisals*, 303.

Application

An appraiser is retained to analyze the feasibility of developing a vacant tract with a garden apartment complex containing 100 two-bedroom units. In their design and amenities, the units are to be typical of the market area, which is part of a community of about 140,000. The units will rent for $650 to $750 per month and are to be marketed to moderate-income earners. If this use is feasible, the apartment complex could be developed and ready for lease-up within one year.

Property Productivity Analysis—Step 1 The appraiser determines that the apartment complex is physically possible. The parcel's size and shape, grading, load-bearing capacity of its soil, and accessibility to utility linkups will allow a low-density apartment use. This use is also found to be legally permissible, or compatible with the current zoning. Location analysis further supports an apartment use. The site is four miles from the central business district, and several employment centers are located on an important arterial between it and the CBD. Community retail centers and public schools are within a one-mile radius.

Market Specification—Step 2 After studying the time/distance relationships between the proposed apartment property and employment centers and support facilities as well as the location of competitive multifamily properties, the appraiser concludes that the northeast quadrant of the city represents the market area for the property. Situated along a 10-mile axis, the city covers approximately 80 square miles. Economic base analysis points to strong demand for moderate-income units. The local economy consists of a mix of strong basic or export industry, such as high-technology and manufacturing, and nonbasic industry, with employment in the professions, retailing, construction, and government.[4] This diversified employment base provides a modicum of job stability and promises some measure of job growth. The city has a population of 140,000, of which over 70% are between 15 and 55 years of age, single (20%) or married couples with (35%) or without (15%) children. Persons older than 55 make up 15% of the population.

Demand Analysis and Forecast—Step 3 Current and future demand for the proposed property is determined by demographic analysis. The appraiser relies on census data compiled by the federal government at the beginning of each decade as well as supplementary data based on estimates and forecasts undertaken by individual localities.[5] The market area population is segmented according to household size and income. Household size greatly

---

4. Economists distinguish between basic industry, which draws money into the local economy, and nonbasic industry, which provides services for the work force employed in basic industry.

5. The national census is published by the Bureau of the Census (U.S. Department of Commerce); other population and employment data are available from state, county, and municipal agencies, e.g., departments of regional development/planning, transportation authorities, and chambers of commerce. For a practical understanding of census data, see Anthony Reynolds' review of *Analysis with Local Census Data: Portrait of Change* by Dowell Meyers (San Diego: Academic Press, Inc., Harcourt Brace Jovanovich, 1992) in the January 1993 issue of *The Appraisal Journal*.

affects the value of multifamily housing units. If the average size is three people—i.e., two adults and a child—it is likely that two-bedroom units will have special appeal (as opposed to studio or three- to four-bedroom apartments). The rate of household formation varies with cohort group[6] in the overall population since different age groups form households at different rates. The rate of household formation also varies with income, which is generally a function of age as well. For example, young singles may postpone marriage and remain at home with their parents if they find rents out of reach. The analyst should work with small-area demand data, either public census tracts or proprietary data such as projections of population growth. For an overall metropolitan area, infrastructure development and the availability of vacant land will help determine which communities or quadrants will grow.

Using the worksheet that follows, the analyst enters current and forecast data to develop an estimate of annual market demand. The worksheet consists of five sections. In each section, demand data are further segmented to arrive at an estimate of the specific demand that the subject property is likely to capture. In the first section (steps 1-6), estimates are made of overall demand for multifamily housing units in the city and the market area. The second section (steps 7-9) segments out demand for rental units from overall housing demand. In the third and fourth sections (steps 10-17 and 18-20), that demand is further broken down to determine the segment with household incomes that can afford units in the rental range for subject-type properties. In the fifth section (steps 21-25), the analyst compares the supply inventory with existing and forecast demand to estimate marginal or residual demand. The period it will take for competitive supply and total supply of subject-type properties to absorb or capture marginal demand is calculated. Finally, the analyst forecasts the number of units of marginal demand the subject is likely to capture annually.

Figure 2.1

Worksheet for Forecasting Market Area Demand and Subject Capture

Section 1

1. Population change in the community during the forecast period.

2. Population change in the market area during the forecast period.

3. Average household size in the community during the forecast period.

4. Average household size in the market area during the forecast period.

5. Total new multifamily housing units in demand in the community (divide Step 1 by Step 3).

6. **Total new multifamily housing units in demand in the market area** (divide Step 2 by Step 4).

---

6. A cohort group may include persons within a discrete age range (e.g., five years, such as ages 20-24 years, or 10 years, such as 20-29) or an indefinite range (e.g., all persons over age 65).

Section 2

7. Percentage of demand that will seek multifamily rental units.

8. **Number of multifamily units that will be in demand in the market area during the forecast period** (multiply Step 6 by Step 7).

9. Number of units that will be in demand each year of the forecast period (divide Step 8 by the number of years in the forecast).

Section 3

10. Minimum monthly rent for a unit in the subject property.

11. Annual rent for the subject (multiply Step 10 by 12).

12. Annual rent as a percentage of household income.

13. Estimated household income (divide Step 11 by Step 12).

14. Maximum monthly rent for a unit in the subject property.

15. Annual rent for the subject (multiply Step 14 by 12).

16. Annual rent as a percentage of household income.

17. Estimated household income (divide Step 15 by Step 16).

Section 4

18. **Percentage of multifamily demand that will seek units in a subject-type property** (number of households with incomes between those estimated in Steps 13 and 17 as a percentage of demand for rental units in the market area).

19. **Market area demand for units in a subject-type property** (multiply Step 8 by Step 18).

20. Annual market area demand for units in a subject-type property (divide Step 19 by the number of years in the forecast).

Section 5

21. Market area supply of units in existing or anticipated subject-type properties adjusted for frictional or normal vacancy (5%).

22. **Residual or marginal demand in the market area during the forecast period** (subtract Step 21 from Step 19).

23. Approximate number of years it will take for the supply to lease up, excluding the subject units (divide Step 21 by Step 20).

24. Approximate number of years it will take total supply to lease up, including the subject units (divide the total of Step 21 plus the number of subject units by Step 20).

25. **Subject capture rate** (Several methods may be applied depending on the situation: where the subject is anticipated to capture a proportionate or pro rata share of demand, this share can be determined by dividing 100% by the number of multifamily projects in the market area; where this is not the case, a competitive rating method may be used to estimate subject capture.)

On the basis of the following historic and projected data, the analyst is able to forecast population growth and average household size for the city and market area.

Year	City Population	Market Area Population	As % of City Population	Market Area Growth	As % of City Growth
1980	91,655	16,498	18.0		
1990	120,985	22,382	18.5	5,884	20.0
1998	140,342	28,068	20.0	5,686	29.4
2003*	169,463	34,740	20.5	6,672	22.9

* The data for year 2003 are based on projections.

Household size for the city and market area can be estimated by dividing the above population data by the number of households.

Year	Households in City	Household Size for City	Households in Market Area	Household Size for Market Area
1980	32,734	2.8	5,935	2.78
1990	44,155	2.74	8,229	2.72
1998	51,978	2.7	10,434	2.69
2003*	63,469	2.67	13,060	2.66

* The data for year 2003 are based on projections.

The analyst enters these data into the first section of the worksheet.

Section 1 of Worksheet for Forecasting Market Area Demand and Subject Capture
1. Population change in the community during the forecast. **29,121**
2. Population change in the market area during the forecast. **6,672**
3. Average household size in the community during the forecast. **2.67**
4. Average household size in the market area during the forecast. **2.66**
5. Total new multifamily housing units in demand in the community (divide Step 1 by Step 3). **29,121/2.67 = 10,907**
6. **Total new multifamily housing units in demand in the market area** (divide Step 2 by Step 4). **6,672/2.66 = 2,508**

The analyst examines data on households in the market area according to distribution by property type. The available data indicate that the distribution has remained stable over the past decade. This distribution is as follows:

- Single-family owner occupancy, 62%

- Condominiums, 7%

- Mobile homes, 1%

- Multifamily rental units, 30%

Using this information, the analyst completes the second section of the worksheet.

Section 2 of Worksheet for Forecasting Market Area Demand and Subject Capture

7. Percentage of demand that will seek multifamily rental units.   **30%**

8. **Number of multifamily units that will be in demand in the market area during the forecast period** (multiply Step 6 by Step 7).   **2,508 x 30% = 752**

9. Number of units that will be in demand each year of the forecast period (divide Step 8 by the number of years in the forecast).   **150**

The analyst knows that the apartments in the subject property are anticipated to rent for between $650 and $750 a month and that the average household spends 27% of its income on housing. Using these data, the analyst completes steps 10 through 17 of the worksheet.

Section 3 of Worksheet for Forecasting Market Area Demand and Subject Capture

10. Minimum monthly rent for a unit in the subject property.   **$650**

11. Annual rent for the subject (multiply Step 10 by 12).   **$7,800**

12. Annual rent as a percentage of household income.   **27%**

13. Estimated household income (divide Step 11 by Step 12).   **$28,900**

14. Maximum monthly rent for a unit in the subject property.   **$750**

15. Annual rent for the subject (multiply Step 14 by 12)   **$9,000**

16. Annual rent as a percentage of household income.   **27%**

17. Estimated household income (divide Step 15 by Step 16).   **$33,300**

The analyst next examines proprietary data on the income distribution of population in the market area for 1998.

Income	Number of Households	As Percentage of Total Households	Percentage in Multifamily Housing	Estimated Number of New Multifamily Units in Demand
Under $10,000	1,123	4%	8%	60
$10,000-$14,999	1,684	6%	12%	90
$15,000-$24,999	3,087	11%	15%	113
$25,000-$34,999	5,062	18%	35%	263
$35,000-$49,999	5,333	19%	30%	226
$45,000-$74,999	6,165	22%		
$75,000 and over	5,614	20%		
Totals	28,068	100%	100%	752*

* The 752 is the number of multifamily units expected to be in demand during the forecast period (2,508 market area demand x the 30% of demand that will seek multifamily housing = 752).

The income range targeted ($28,900-$33,300) is within the $25,000-$34,999 bracket. The bracket overlap includes households that pay a higher or lower percentage of their income toward rent. The analyst selects the percentage of households in this income bracket that are most likely to seek units in subject-type properties and enters it in the worksheet.

Section 4 of Worksheet for Forecasting Market Area Demand and Subject Capture

18. **Percentage of multifamily demand that will seek units in a subject-type property** (number of households with incomes between $28,900 and $33,300 as a percentage of demand for rental units in the market area).   **35%**

19. **Market area demand for units in a subject-type property** (multiply Step 8 by Step 18).   **752 x 35% = 263**

20. Annual market area demand for units in a subject-type property (divide Step 19 by the number of years in the forecast).   **263/5 = 53**

Competitive Supply Analysis and Forecast—Step 4   The next step is to inventory the existing and anticipated supply of subject-type properties in the market area, i.e., under construction or in planning. Vacant units in existing apartments and buildings pending completion are estimated. To evaluate the likelihood of more units being added to the anticipated stock, the analyst considers factors such as financing and construction costs, which directly influence multifamily housing starts. Supply may be affected by rent controls specifying the maximum rent for units in an apartment building. Rent controls ultimately affect the supply of apartment properties by discouraging potential buyers and developers. Another item to investigate is whether any apartment buildings may be undergoing condominium or cooperative conversion. These will be lost to the immediate competitive supply.

The inventory of existing and anticipated units is adjusted for the frictional or normal vacancy rate in the community. The frictional vacancy rate is unrelated to any structural disequilibrium in supply and demand. Rather it reflects the normal vacancy level resulting from tenant turnover.

The analyst compiles the following inventory of units in apartment buildings developed in the past five years. The three buildings are highly similar to the proposed subject in amenities and accessibility.

Supply of Existing Competitive Apartment Space

Apartment Building	Total Units	Total Units less Frictional Vacancy (5%)	Units Rented	Available Units
Savoy	150	143	138	5
Stratford	200	190	180	10
Plaza	250	238	225	13
Total	600	571	543	28

Supply of Forecast Competitive Apartment Space

Apartment Building under Construction	Total Units	Anticipated Completion Date and Availability
Bellevue	50	25 to be phased in at 3 months and 9 months

Equilibrium Analysis—Step 5   Currently, 28 units are available, to which 25 new units will be added in three months, and another 25 units in nine months. If the subject is developed, 100 additional units will augment supply at the end of this year. Thus, a total of 178 units will be available at the end of this year. Anticipated annual demand for units in subject type apartment projects is 53 (step 20). The remaining steps of the worksheet can now be completed.

Section 5 of Worksheet for Forecasting Market Area Demand and Subject Capture

21. Market area supply of units in existing or anticipated subject-type properties, after adjustment for 5% frictional or normal vacancy. **178**

22. **Residual or marginal demand in the market area during the forecast period** (subtract Step 21 from Step 19). **263 - 178 = 85**

23. Approximate number of years it will take for the supply to lease up, excluding the subject units (divide Step 21 by Step 20). **78/53 = 1½ years**

24. Approximate number of years it will take total supply to lease up, including the subject units (divide the total of Step 21 plus the number of subject units by Step 20). **178/53 = 3⅓ years**
(The subject units, however, will not be available until the end of year 1; therefore, the absorption period will extend longer.)

25. **Subject capture rate.** (The subject is anticipated to capture a proportionate or pro rata share of demand once it is completed, at the beginning of year 2.)

Subject Capture—Step 6   In the first year, the four multifamily projects in the market can each be expected to absorb 25% of the 53-unit annual demand. Since the pro rata shares of this demand are larger than the absorption capacity of the three existing projects, the shortfall will be captured by the fourth project's adding 50 new units to market supply by the end of year 1. Also note that once the existing projects achieve stabilized occupancy, they no longer continue to absorb shares of marginal demand. Thus, in the second and third years, the percentage allocation changes to 33⅓% and 50%.

Forecast Apartment Project Absorption

Name of Complex	Vacant and Available Units Start of Year 1	Vacant and Available Units End of Year 1	Vacant and Available Units Start of Year 2	Vacant and Available Units End of Year 2
	(Each will capture 25% of the 53 units in demand)		*(Each will capture 50% of the 53 units in demand)*	
Savoy	5	0	0	0
Stratford	10	0	0	0
Plaza	13	0	0	0
Bellevue	0	25 (53 - 28)	25	0
Subject	0	100	100 (100 - 28)	72

Name of Complex	Vacant and Available Units Start of Year 3 *(Subject will capture all of the 53 units in demand)*	Vacant and Available Units End of Year 3	Vacant and Available Units Start of Year 4 *(Subject's remaining 19 units will lease up)*	Vacant and Available Units End of Year 4
Subject	72 (72 - 53)	19	19	0

Provided that the number of competitive units remains the same, the subject will achieve a level of stabilized occupancy in the fifth year of the forecast and the fourth year after the subject units became available.

Financial Feasibility Analysis

Two other potential uses of the site are development as a subdivision for residential properties or as a multitenant professional building. Market analysis indicates that support exists for both alternative uses. Therefore, it is necessary to determine which of the three uses is maximally profitable. Residual land values, rates of return, and capitalized values of the property under each of the uses can be estimated and used as criteria for analyzing financial feasibility.

Residual Land Values　The estimated costs of development, including construction and marketing but excluding land, may be deducted from the anticipated gross sale price or capitalized *NOI* expectancy to provide an indication of the net sale proceeds or net cash flows upon a specified future date, e.g., sellout or stabilized occupancy. The present value of total net sale proceeds or net cash flows over the development and marketing period will provide an indication of the residual value of the raw land.[8] Residual values of the land under alternative uses can then be compared. In a procedure known as *threshold testing,*[9] a use is tested with especially optimistic forecast data in order to give it every chance of succeeding. If the residual land value under the given use does not compare favorably with other uses, it is eliminated from further consideration.

Rates of Return　The analyst may also forecast absorption or lease-up and discount future cash flows (net sale proceeds or net operating income) to estimate the internal rate of return (*IRR*)[10] to the property under each use (the internal rate of return is the rate of discount that makes the net present value equal to zero). If the internal rate of return under a given use is equal to or greater than the typical rate required by investors, or minimum threshold rate, the use qualifies as financially feasible.[11] Among alternative uses, the use that results in the highest rate of return, provided all the risks are comparable, is the highest and best use.

---

8. *The Appraisal of Real Estate*, 11th ed. (Chicago: Appraisal Institute, 1996), 328-331.

9. Stephen F. Fanning, Terry V. Grissom, and Thomas D. Pearson, *Market Analysis for Valuation Appraisals,* 390, 401.

10. Discussion of threshold rates of return in Douglas D. Lovell and Robert S. Martin, *Subdivision Analysis* (Chicago: Appraisal Institute, 1993), 47, 112-114.

11. C.F. Sirmans and Austin Jaffe, *The Complete Real Estate Investment Handbook* (Englewood Cliffs, N.J.: Prentice-Hall, 1985), 18.

Capitalized Property Values Similarly, a future cash flow (net sale proceeds or net operating income) may be directly capitalized into an indication of the value of the overall property at sellout or stabilized occupancy.[12] Property values under each of the alternative uses are compared, and the use that results in the highest value, all risks being comparable, represents the highest and best use.

In the above example, the analyst compares anticipated rates of return to the three property uses with those required by investors in the market. The minimum required rate for residential subdivision developments is 15%; for multitenant professional buildings, 10%; and for multifamily housing projects, 12%. The appraiser estimates the rate of return for a proposed subdivision at 11.5% and for a proposed multitenant professional building, 9%. However, the proposed multifamily housing project will yield a rate of return of 12.5%. The rate of return for the proposed multifamily housing project exceeds the minimum required by investors in the market, whereas the rates for the proposed residential subdivision and multitenant office building fall short of market requirements.

---

12. *The Appraisal of Real Estate,* 11th ed., 309-311.

CHAPTER 3

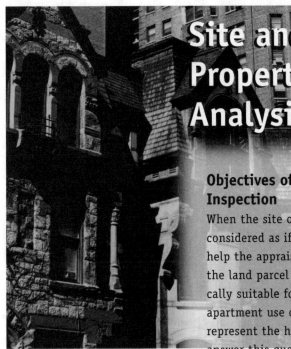

Site and Property Analysis

Objectives of Site and Property Inspection

When the site of the property is vacant or being considered as if vacant, the site inspection will help the appraiser determine the extent to which the land parcel is physically, legally, and economically suitable for apartment development. Does an apartment use of the type and density proposed represent the highest and best use of the site? To answer this question, the appraiser gathers the following information during the inspection: the dimensions and area of the site, its accessibility and grading, the local zoning, the available utilities/site improvements, their compliance with zoning and building codes, and the site location. With this information, the appraiser forms a judgment on whether the site is suitable for the proposed development.

For existing apartment properties, the inspection is undertaken to gather descriptive information on the physical characteristics of the improvements, including a quality and condition survey of all building components and an analysis of the functional utility of the property in terms of its design, energy systems, and amenities. This information also relates to the highest and best use of the property. It is analyzed to determine whether the improved property should be maintained as is, or renovated, expanded, or possibly partly or

In an older urban environment, density is a major determinant of highest and best use.

totally demolished. Since apartment buildings are income-producing properties, any further capital expenditure must be justified by an anticipated increase in revenue.

The property inspection is critical not only to the conclusion of highest and best use for the property but also to the collection of data used in selecting comparables. The analysis of the subject property suggests the features to study in comparable properties, e.g., siting, land-to-building ratio, location, site accessibility, density of development, level of maintenance, quality and condition of building components, and functional utility. Because comparable properties provide data the appraiser needs to apply all three approaches to value, the property inspection plays a pivotal role. The time and effort spent on the inspection will vary with the size and complexity of the apartment property.

Site Analysis

Site analysis includes two principal steps. The first is a review of title and record data to obtain a legal description of the property as well as information on the property ownership, assessments, and any public or private restrictions that limit property use such as zoning, land use provisions (in deeds), easements, or other encumbrances. The second is the field inspection to examine the physical characteristics of the site, adequacy of utilities and services, locational and environmental influences, and site improvements. This is where the appraiser identifies the advantages or disadvantages that affect the site's marketability.

Review of Title and Record Data

Property Address and Legal Description　　The appraiser should obtain and reference a complete street address of the building(s) and identify the apartment building or complex by name, if appropriate. In many areas, an assessor's lot and block number is commonly cited. If the site is vacant, a more formal means of identification may be required. Because large apartment developments are often constructed and financed in phases, it is important to ascertain whether the entire development is to be appraised or, if not, the extent to which the parts of the development not being appraised affect the use of the parts that are.

A legal description specifically identifies the land parcel, its size, recorded easements, and other site data. Legal descriptions are based on precise surveys. Maintained as public records in accordance with local and state laws, legal descriptions are found in deed files, in the public recorder's office, or among the documents kept by the property owner. The legal description should be read carefully and compared against the subject site before it is referenced or included in the appraisal report. The legal description must be verified to ensure that it corresponds to the subject land parcel and accurately describes it. For appraisals of medium- to large-scale apartment complexes, clients often furnish a preliminary title report. This provides the appraiser with a site map, legal description, and data concerning easements, rights of way, or reservations. It is common practice to reference this document in the text and enclose a complete copy in the addenda of the report.

Ownership Information　　Information on the legal owner and type of ownership is available from public records maintained by a county clerk or from local title or abstract companies. If the property is held in fee simple ownership, a direct statement to this effect is generally sufficient for the appraisal report. If a leasehold or land lease is involved, the appraiser should describe the terms of the relevant lease and report its effect on the marketability of the property and its value.

The Uniform Standards of Professional Appraisal Practice (USPAP) require that an appraiser consider and analyze any current agreement of sale, option, or listing of the property if such information is available to the appraiser in the normal course of business. Also to be considered is any prior sale of the subject property over the previous year for one- to four-family residential units and three years for all other property types.[1]

Apartment projects fall under the three-year rule. The intention of these provisions is to require the investigation, analysis, and reporting of any prior sales or marketing activity that bears on the valuation of the subject property as of the effective date of the appraisal.

Zoning and Land Use Provisions   Zoning sets the minimum requirements to which buildings erected on a site must conform. General residential zoning categories typically correspond to building density. For example, one series of zoning categories may include the following:

- R-1   Single-family residences

- R-2   Two- to three-unit buildings

- R-3   Low- to medium-density apartment buildings with fewer than 25 units

- R-4   Medium- to high-density apartment buildings with 25 to 50 units

- R-5   High-density and/or high-rise apartment buildings with more than 50 units

When zoning restrictions limit the density of use by specifying setbacks, off-street parking requirements, building height, and floor area ratios, the capacity of the site to accommodate dwelling unit space is impaired.

In conducting a site analysis, the appraiser considers the number of dwelling units or square footage of building that the existing zoning allows or proposed zoning would allow on the site. To provide a basis for the conclusion of highest and best use, the appraiser compares the maximum number of units legally permitted and economically justifiable with the number actually built or proposed and with the densities of competitive apartment projects. If the appraiser believes the subject site has too few apartments, further analysis is undertaken to determine whether building additional units is physically possible and legally permissible.

If rent controls are in place or proposed, their effect upon the value of the apartment property should be investigated. Such controls may extend to tenant rights concerning eviction, apartment house rules, and purchase of units in the project.

---

1. Uniform Standards of Professional Appraisal Practice (USPAP) (Washington, D.C.: The Appraisal Foundation, 1998), Standards Rule 1-5 (a) and (b).

In areas subject to floods, earthquakes, and other natural hazards, regulations often limit construction. In coastal and historic districts, zoning and other provisions may govern building location and design.

Off-street parking requirements are a major consideration in the valuation of apartment properties. Ordinances stipulating the ratio of parking stalls per residential unit and the average minimum size of each space affect project development costs and maximum occupancy potential. The amount and type of off-street parking provided for tenants and their guests may directly influence the rental income that the apartment units can generate.

When site valuation is the purpose of the appraisal or when development of an apartment project is proposed, the appraiser should personally interview municipal planning and zoning staff. It is essential to understand how regulations apply to the property and the permissibility of existing and potential uses of the site. Because many zoning and land use regulations are not listed in the recorded title to the property, confirmation from the controlling agency or agencies becomes necessary.

Tax and Assessment Information   Real property taxes are based on ad valorem assessments. The records of the county assessor or tax collector can provide the details of a property's assessed value and annual tax burden. From the present assessment data and recent history of tax rates, the appraiser can formulate conclusions about future taxes. Property taxes directly increase the cost of ownership and therefore reduce the net income derived from the rental of apartment units. The fairness of the assessment and anticipated future taxes must be thoroughly analyzed and their impact on value considered in the property appraisal. Property taxes are generally imposed to pay for local government services such as fire fighting, police protection, and schools. Apartment properties in well-run communities, however, will attract potential tenants willing to pay higher rents for the superior services provided.

Special assessments are levied to pay for infrastructure development (roads or utilities) and extraordinary services (fire or police protection). Ideally, the value of the properties subject to special assessment is not penalized. The enhancement resulting from the new infrastructure or the provision of additional services should offset the tax increase. However, when a property is subject to a special assessment that exceeds the benefit derived, the value of the property is diminished.

Deed and Easement Restrictions   Deed restrictions, which generally run with the title to land as it is conveyed from one owner to another, can limit the type, size, and character of the building improvement constructed on the site. While observance may initially be voluntary, once the deed restriction becomes publicly recorded it effectively limits the present and future use of the site as well as its present and future owners.

An easement is an arrangement whereby the property owner retains legal title to the real property but conveys to another party an interest in that property, such as a right of way or a right to use a specific part of the site to access an adjoining property. Surface easements are the most common, but many other types, such as subterranean and overhead easements, are used for public utility connections and underground transit service. A property that acquires an easement (the dominant estate) is a beneficiary, whereas one that is subject to an easement (the servient estate) is burdened or encumbered. Existing easements can affect the utility of a site. For example, an apartment site is encumbered by a 25-foot-wide underground utility easement running diagonally across its rear yard. Because the easement prohibits construction of a swimming pool or another common area improvement, the apartment site incurs a significant loss in value.

Since most appraisers are not qualified to practice law, their ability to identify and quantify all legal restrictions affecting a site is limited. In reporting a valuation, it is advisable to include a statement that apart from those identified within the report, the appraiser assumes there to be no easements, restrictions, or legal conditions in effect that would negatively affect the value of the appraised property.

Site Characteristics

Size and Shape   In describing the dimensions of the land parcel, the appraiser notes its frontage, width, and depth. If the site is irregularly configured, the frontage will not be the same as the width of the site. A regularly configured land parcel is better suited to apartment development. Frontage should be adequate but not excessive, and depth should be sufficient to allow the tenants privacy and protection from noise. For an apartment property site to be maximally profitable, it must optimally accommodate the apartment complex that stands on it.

Site area helps determine the possible uses of the site. Buildable area, sometimes referred to as *usable* or *effective* area, is the part of the land parcel on which building construction may take place. Buildable area is estimated by subtracting from total site or gross area those sections of the site that are physically unsuitable for building or unusable sections subject to easements, zoning setbacks, and deed restrictions. The difference between gross area and effective area may or may not affect the value of an apartment property site. Where allowable building density is calculated as a ratio of gross land area to gross building space, a reduced effective area does not necessarily diminish utility. But in some situations, the legally permissible density exceeds the limit of economically prudent development. A site large enough to allow the apartment complex "to create its own environment" may accrue a value premium.

Plottage and Excess Land   In some cases, the highest and best use of a land parcel is for it to be assembled with one or more other land parcels into a single development site. If the combined parcels have a greater unit value after assemblage, plottage value is created. For example, apartment buildings in a dynamic rental district typically contain 20 to 40 units. Several factors account for this being the most profitable type of residential rental development in the district, among them economies of construction, the flexibility of design, and the appeal of the size and unit mix. Under current zoning regulations, the subject lot can accommodate only 15 units. Assemblage with an adjacent parcel to create a single development site will allow construction of a 30-unit building and result in a higher unit value for the combined parcels than the parcels would have if they remained separate.

Some vacant sites include excess land not needed to accommodate their highest and best use or land that exceeds the standard lot size in the market. Improved sites may have excess land not needed to support the existing building improvements. Excess land will sometimes support future expansion of the existing improvement. Or, if legally and effectively marketable, it can be a separate development site.

Topography   Topography encompasses the land parcel's contour, grade, elevation in relation to adjacent rights-of-way, soil conditions, natural drainage, installed drainage systems, and general utility. Extreme topography adds to building costs and tends to penalize site value. An apartment site that is higher or lower than the abutting street may create additional costs to construct foundations or correct drainage and accessibility problems. But the excess cost is sometimes more than offset by the additional rent that can be obtained for the apartments offering a scenic view or greater privacy.

Soil/subsoil stability or bearing capacity affects the cost of preparing the site for construction as well as the design and placement of the complex to be developed. If there is any concern about the suitability of the soil, an engineering study of its bearing capacity is usually commissioned. Drainage depends on the topography and ability of the soil to absorb water. The storm sewer system is especially important. An apartment project with a basement or parking cellars must have drains to carry the water out from under the structure and to prevent leaks from developing. Special precautions must be taken for apartments constructed on a slope to keep run-off water away from the sides of the building. If the project is located in a designated flood hazard area, it is necessary to consider whether any of the topographical features of the site increase or decrease its susceptibility to flooding.

Utilities and Service   Water, electricity, natural or liquid petroleum (propane) gas, sewage, trash collection, street maintenance, telephone, and cable television are essential utilities and services in most residential markets. If the utilities on the site are inadequate, the cost of improving utility service must be considered. Utilities may be publicly provided or privately owned as part of a community system. In some cases, utilities are individual to the site. The availability and reliability of utilities have a direct bearing on the amount of rent a tenant will pay. At the same time, the cost of utility services is an operating expense that affects the potential net income of the project. The effect of this expenditure is investigated by comparing the costs of utilities and services at competing buildings in relation to rents with the costs incurred by the subject.

Locational and Environmental Influences   Another element to analyze is whether the immediate environment of the subject property is suitable for the type of apartment development. A project consisting primarily of efficiency or studio units will appeal to career-oriented singles. The highest rents and occupancy levels will be obtained if the property is located in or near the downtown, close to work centers and public transit. For occupants of low-rent units or elderly housing, access to transportation and shopping areas is especially important, as is proximity to schools for tenants with children. In medium- to high-rent apartment districts, tenants seek not only ease of accessibility but also neighborhood amenities such as trendy restaurants and other entertainment or recreational facilities.

Lot Type and Orientation   Common types of apartment property sites include interior, corner, cul-de-sac, and flag or pipe stem lots. Most multifamily projects are built on interior lots with frontage on only one street. The main access is from the street, although rear alleys can also provide ingress and egress. In describing the location of such a property, the appraiser notes the distance and direction from the nearest intersection. A corner lot has frontage on and can be accessed from two or more streets. Corner location has advantages and disadvantages—increased light and air but more noise and congestion from passing traffic. Does a corner location reduce or enhance the site's marketability in comparison with competing sites? It depends on the market.

Cul-de-sac lots are located at the end of dead-end streets where circular turnaround areas are common. A flag lot is a long, narrow rear parcel with limited access. Cul-de-sac and flag lots used for apartment properties allow for privacy and distance from traffic. They appeal to renters with children.

Access and Street Maintenance   Tenants also consider the ease or difficulty of access in selecting an apartment. Access may be via a public street, a right-of-way over abutting property, or a private drive. Many lenders require the project to front on a publicly dedicated and maintained street that meets community standards. Information on the maintenance of the access street or road should be analyzed. If the street or drive is privately owned, there must be a legally enforceable agreement governing its maintenance.

Hazards and Nuisances   Proximity to the noise, congestion, and fumes of heavy traffic can penalize the value of an apartment project. Rentals of two- to three-bedroom apartments are especially affected since families with small children prefer to live a distance away from the hazards of traffic. Potential flooding is receiving more attention from appraisers because of lender requirements concerning flood zone identification and flood insurance. The Federal Emergency Management Agency (FEMA) publishes lists of districts identified as flood hazard areas. The presence of hazardous materials that can cause serious illness and environmental degradation has also become a primary consideration in the purchase and rental of residential property. Warning signs to look for during the site inspection include, but are certainly not limited to, oily sheen or puddles in drainage ditches, discolored vegetation, and drums that possibly contain paints, coolants, or solvents. The appraiser should consider competitive properties in assessing the effect of nuisances and hazards. The due diligence process for the inspection of residential properties prescribed by the Appraisal Institute and its Guide Note 8, The Consideration of Hazardous Substances in the Appraisal Process, are discussed in the next section, Property Analysis.

The proximity of support facilities—e.g., convenience stores, retail centers, restaurants, entertainment, and recreational facilities—contributes to the value of an apartment site but may penalize its marketability if located too close. In outlying districts, reasonable proximity to gas stations, public schools, fire houses, and convenience stores is desirable. Uses that do not mix well or do not conform to community standards negatively affect rent levels.

View and Climate   Because a scenic view is a major consideration to many tenants, rents tend to increase with floor level in apartment buildings. The appraiser should consider the likelihood of the property's existing views being obstructed in the future. View easements, tract restrictions, or city/county ordinances may serve as protection. If a particular site is influenced by special climatic conditions, such as fog or wind, the value may be affected.

Site Improvements   Site improvements refer to both the preparation of the site for a proposed building (excavation, leveling and grading, filling and compacting) and the actual state of finished site improvements with an existing property (driveways, parking, walks, retaining walls, patios, and recreational facilities). Finished site improvements are appraised on the basis of their contribution to project value.

A major factor in apartment building design and construction, parking is analyzed in terms of the number and type of dwelling units and the requirements of the typical tenants. A parking ratio is the number of off-street parking spaces divided by the number of dwelling units. If 220 parking stalls have been built for a 100-unit apartment complex, the parking ratio is 2.2. Parking ratios vary from region to region and market to market, as does the type of parking facility—e.g., open lot, covered carport, or enclosed underground garage. The available parking should be identified by type. Covered facilities or garage parking spaces are generally required for higher rent properties. The appraiser will calculate the gross area of visitor and tenant parking, the number of stalls, and the ratio of spaces to apartment units. The standard parking space is 9 feet by 18 feet; for compact cars, the space is 8.25 feet by 17.5 feet. Spaces for handicapped occupants need to be larger. In self-park garages, the required area per vehicle ranges from 300 to 350 square feet.

Larger apartment complexes often include project amenities such as community buildings, storage lockers, and recreational facilities. Many of these amenities are appraised as structures in the same manner as building improvements.

Property Analysis

In an in-depth study of the apartment development, the size is calculated and the style, design, and layout of the building(s) are identified. This analysis includes examination of the construction quality and level of maintenance as well as a description of the building components, materials, and mechanical systems, including the quality and condition of each component. The appraiser will take note of common areas, common facilities or amenities, unit mix, unit size and count, and room count. Two other factors that are critical to the upkeep, operation, and thus the income generation of the property are the property management and the tenancy.

Property Management

Building size determines the type of management. Generally, buildings of more than 25 units are of sufficient size to bear the additional burden of professional property management; larger high-rise or garden apartment projects of over 50 units often require the additional services of a site or resident manager. Lenders generally prefer that properties be professionally managed.

A property manager reports to the property owners, sets rent levels, establishes marketing procedures, and does the fiscal planning for the project. The property manager also supervises on-site employees, among whom the resident manager is responsible for looking after the day-to-day dealings with the tenants, leasing of units, collection of rents, and coordination of routine and long-term building maintenance. The resident manager may oversee janitorial staff, an on-site maintenance crew, or various outside contractors. Large-scale apartment projects and newly built developments also employ leasing agents to fill vacancies or negotiate lease renewals and to assist with marketing programs, promotion, and advertising.

For the appraiser, the property manager is an invaluable source of primary data. Resident managers and leasing agents can also provide critical information on the income and expense history of the property, current leasing activity, tenant profiles, rent rolls, and the physical characteristics of the building.

Tenant Profile

Real estate agents and property managers classify tenants under two categories. Tenants by choice are those who choose to live in rental units; tenants by circumstance are those who must seek rental accommodations either because their lives are in some degree of flux or they cannot yet afford to purchase a house. Tenants by choice usually sign a formal lease, occupy their unit for an extended period, and cause fewer problems for the management. Tenants by choice are mostly empty nesters (older couples whose children are grown), career-oriented persons (singles or couples), and retired persons or senior citizens. Tenants by circumstance are more transitory, have less commitment to keeping up their apartments, and are less likely to invest effort or money on creating a formal, homelike environment.[2]

---

2. In the past, furnished apartments made up a large segment of the multifamily market. With the greater availability of credit, most tenants are now able to purchase furniture and appliances on installment plans. Or tenants may often rent furniture. Whereas renting furnished units can be a burden on management and long-term drain on net income, in limited situations it may be justified economically, for example, housing for college students or seasonal occupants in resort or vacation areas. Because furniture is personal property, the sale price of an occasional comparable property with furnished units will require adjustment.

Tenants by circumstance include out-of-town students, singles who have recently entered the job market, and families with young children. Whereas families with young children tend to be less mobile, students generally lease for short tenancies and singles lacking job security may vacate on short notice. Students and singles often give rise to collection losses.

The property manager should be questioned about how prospective tenants are screened, the types of jobs the tenants hold, their parking requirements, and the average number of evictions and tenant turnover on a yearly basis.

Building Appearance and Marketability

Exterior appearance is critical because a prospective tenant forms an initial impression of the property based on its "curb appeal." Thus, the property inspection begins with the overall exterior appearance and what it tells about the condition, maintenance, style, and age of the structure. The exterior inspection should alert the appraiser to any major repairs that have been deferred or items in need of attention.

The interior inspection provides an inventory of area measurements (gross building area, gross leasable area, net leasable area) and the number and size of the rental units in the project. Items to note include the layout, interior placement or orientation of the units, utility of design, quality of fixtures, and any amenity features that command optimal rents. The inspection also covers the condition of the finish hardware (hinges, locks, and door-knobs), plumbing and energy systems (electrical system, HVAC, and hot water), elevators, and common areas such as entranceways, halls, basements, laundry rooms, and recreational facilities. This interior inspection reveals the age and condition of building machinery and equipment as well as items of deferred maintenance or curable obsolescence and any noncompliance with building ordinances.

Unit Size, Design, and Utility

Apartments within a building generally vary according to size, room number, and layout. The distribution or allocation of the various types is known as the *unit mix*. For example, a development of 100 apartments may contain 50 units with one bedroom and one bath, 30 units with two bedrooms and two baths, and 20 units with three bedrooms and two baths. The square footage will vary from one base model to another; apartments with the same number of rooms may also be of different sizes if the models are not all the same design. To rate the efficiency and utility of the project requires judging the compatibility of the apartment types and determining how well the subject unit mix competes in the market. An optimum unit mix is achieved when the project is properly conceived with respect to its location and intended tenants. Nevertheless, changing economic conditions can adversely affect the desirability of particular unit sizes. Because no one unit size can be expected to attract the same level of demand indefinitely, developers generally ensure a unit mix adequate to maintain stable occupancy levels over extended periods.

Area Calculations

The analysis of the unit mix depends on the reliable measurement of building and unit areas as well as an accurate room count. The most common measure is gross building area (GBA), or the total floor area of a building, excluding unenclosed areas, measured from the exterior of the walls.[3] Included in total floor area are common areas (interior stairways, corridors, storage units) and below-grade space (basements). A second important measure is net leasable area (NLA) or net rentable area (NRA), the amount of space rented to the individual tenants, excluding common areas.[4] The ratio of net leasable area to gross building area is known as the building's *efficiency factor.* For example, an apartment project with a gross building area of 100,000 square feet and net leasable area of 90,000 square feet has an efficiency factor of 90%. Because of a greater proportion of interior common area, large entrance areas, and space for machinery and equipment, high-rise and mid-rise developments usually have an efficiency factor in the 80% to 85% range.

Apartment valuation calls for the following calculations: the gross building area, the net leasable area, and the efficiency ratio as well as the gross square footage of each building in the complex, each floor, and the basement or subbasement (if any). The leasable area for each type of unit is also required, as is the average area per unit (net leasable area divided by the total number of units).

Unit and Room Count

The number of units and number of rooms per unit are calculated in each valuation. The unit count includes all apartments in the building being appraised, including those occupied by the owner or manager. The room count reflects the size, area, and layout of each unit. Apartment sizes are distinguished by the number of bedrooms and bathrooms as well as the total number of rooms in the unit. A kitchen, regardless of its size, is always considered as one room. A bathroom that contains a bathtub or shower stall, a toilet, and a wash basin (three fixtures) is considered a full bath, but it is **not** included in the room count. A half-bath generally consists of two fixtures—a basin and a toilet. A living room and full dining room are counted as one room each. A living/dining room combination is usually considered 1½ rooms, unless the combined space exceeds 300 square feet, in which case it could be subdivided. To ensure consistency, the appraiser must be careful to apply the same method of counting to the subject and comparable properties.

---

3. *The Appraisal of Real Estate,* 11th ed., 243. No national standard exists for measuring multifamily housing as does for single-family houses and office buildings—i.e., the voluntary standard adopted in 1994 by the American National Standards Institute (ANSI) together with the National Association of Homebuilders (NAHB), or the standard for measuring floor area in office buildings, which was developed in 1915 and subsequently revised by the Building Owners and Managers Association (BOMA).

4. Stephen F. Fanning, Terry V. Grissom, and Thomas D. Pearson, *Market Analysis for Valuation Appraisals,* 304.

Project Amenities

Project amenities fall into two categories: recreational facilities and support facilities. The value of recreational features such as swimming pools, saunas, tennis courts, gazebos, and communal rooms/buildings depends on the overall size and character of the development as well as facilities available in competitive properties. Such features must be rated against facilities in competitive developments.

Support facilities are amenities that meet basic tenant needs, such as vending machines, laundry rooms, storage areas, and security systems. Soft drink, candy, and ice dispensers usually occupy a separate room near a recreation area or laundry room, inconspicuous but easy to access. Laundry rooms are likely to contain single-load washers and dryers, a laundry basin, and a sorting table. The number of washers and dryers depends on the number of units and the typical tenant in occupancy. In buildings rented to young families and career people, approximately one washer and one dryer are required for each 10 to 15 apartments. Because fewer occupants of high-rent complexes do their own laundry, the ratio in luxury buildings falls to one washer/dryer for every 20 to 30 units.

Storage facilities should be well lit, secure, ample in size, and identified by the tenant's name or apartment number. In larger apartment complexes, the storage facility is often located in the garage area in front of the tenant's reserved parking space. In especially luxurious apartments, individual storage units are situated in airtight and locked utility rooms on various floors or in the basement. Security systems may rely on electronic surveillance via television monitors or on-site personnel. Luxury suburban garden apartments often employ gatekeepers; doormen serve this function in urban high-rise complexes. Apartment buildings also make use of dead-bolt locks, apartment-to-lobby intercom systems, or devices that allow tenants to screen callers.

Environmental Conditions

Under current standards, an appraiser is responsible for noting in the appraisal report any environmental hazards either "known" through normal research involved in the appraisal or "observed" during the course of the property inspection, and commenting on any influence the hazard has on the value and marketability of the property.[5] Although the typical real estate appraiser is neither expected nor required to be an environmental specialist, the reporting of any and all adverse conditions is a basic responsibility. When there is no reason to believe the property is affected by hazardous substances, appraisers are advised to include a standard disclaimer or limiting condition concerning hazardous substances in their appraisal reports.

---

5. Uniform Standards of Professional Appraisal Practice (USPAP), 1998, Advisory Opinion AO-9, Responsibility of Appraisers Concerning Toxic or Hazardous Substance Consideration (adopted 1992), and the Appraisal Institute's Guide Notes to the Standards of Professional Appraisal Practice, Guide Note 8, "The Consideration of Hazardous Substances in the Appraisal Process" (1991/1994). The Property Observation Checklist, adopted by the Appraisal Institute in 1995, is consistent with the advisory opinion and guide note. Use of the checklist, however, is voluntary.

Asbestos-containing materials (ACMs) were commonly used in construction between 1945 and 1970 to insulate walls and pipes. ACMs can become carcinogenic when the asbestos fibers become airborne through crumbling or pulverizing. Urea-formaldehyde foam, used during the 1960s and 1970s, was intermittently banned in construction during the 1980s. The appraiser should inquire about the possible presence of walls covered with lead-based paints or plumbing lines that contain lead. In particular, basements, storage areas, and garages should be checked during the property inspection for evidence of hazardous substances.

Special Considerations
Nonconforming Uses

Many apartment buildings constructed before 1960 do not comply with current building codes. The cost required to renovate such structures or bring them up to code can represent a considerable problem for the owner or potential buyer. Yet if this is not done, financing may not be available. A legally nonconforming use is usually created by the imposition of zoning or a change in zoning after the original construction was completed. Examples of noncompliance include existing complexes with more units than are permitted under the current zoning, properties that do not provide adequate parking under the existing ordinance, or those that do not comply with building regulations regarding earthquakes, fire, and other potential hazards.

Some jurisdictions require nonconforming uses to be phased out over a stipulated period. If such a use is discontinued or terminated because of a storm or fire, the degree of damage incurred will determine whether the use can be reestablished. Even where a nonconforming use is permitted, lenders often require insurance for the possible situation in which the building is partially or wholly destroyed and the city requires a replacement that conforms to current code.

A reduction in the permitted density or a change in development standards sometimes makes a legally nonconforming use more valuable. Usually, any bonus resulting from the nonconforming improvement is directly related to the existing building. When a zoning change creates a value premium for a nonconforming improvement, continuation of the use may produce more benefits and/or income than would accrue if the improvement were built to current code. In these situations, the property value reflects the nonconforming use. Land value, however, is estimated on the basis of the currently permissible use because in site valuation the land is assumed to be vacant and available for development to its highest and best use as of the effective date of the appraisal.

Condominium Conversion

Conversion of rental apartments to condominiums has become a major real estate activity over the past few years. Some experts believe that in time most well-located, quality-construction rental properties will be converted to sale units. Condominium conversion is not, however, without risk. Not all apartment buildings can be converted and problems are associated with marketing newly converted units. The main cause of failure is that the sponsor underestimates the time and cost required to sell the individual units. The appraiser, therefore, should pay particular attention to forecasting potential absorption and expenses, including the cost of borrowed money and rent losses over the conversion and marketing period.

An analysis of population and income in the subject market is essential to determine the number of potential buyers. This is especially important in the valuation of conversions because the developer cannot simply build to suit the market but rather is constrained by the character of existing apartments and their tenancy. The market analysis is not predicated on what product the typical buyer wants but on whether the given product of existing units has a suitable market. Buildings that have rented well are likely to succeed as condominiums. Since sales to tenants contribute to the success of any conversion, only buildings with low tenant turnover are considered candidates for conversion. A general rule of thumb requires that at least 25% of the existing tenants must be capable of purchasing their apartment units and are willing to do so. Lease expirations should be checked; delays caused by long-term leases increase expenses and defer revenues. An economic advantage is sometimes offered to induce tenants to purchase their apartments. Total monthly occupancy costs, including mortgage payments, real estate taxes, and common area maintenance charges should be comparable to current rents.

High-rise buildings in urban areas are generally considered more suitable for conversion than suburban garden apartments; and middle-income and luxury apartments are better candidates for conversion than low-income properties. The mix of bedrooms is an important factor. Nationally, the greatest demand is for two-bedroom units, while studio, one-bedroom, and larger apartments have more limited appeal. In determining the feasibility of conversion, the appraiser should inspect the building for attributes that enhance marketability or detriments that impair it. These include features such as the building's reputation, the view, balconies and patios, on-site parking, and recreational facilities. Both buyers and long-term lenders are interested in the quality of construction and the amount of deferred maintenance. Well-constructed, well-maintained buildings are better candidates for conversion because of the more favorable ratio between the costs to upgrade and the benefits to be derived from anticipated sale prices. The emphasis in conversion is generally on the enhancement of common areas (carpeting of halls, interior painting, landscaping) as well as the replacement of equipment (boilers, water heaters, elevators) and building cover (roofs and exterior painting). The amount of renovation done on the individual units will depend on the quality and condition of apartments in competitive projects, the anticipated sale prices, and the marketing program.

Cooperative Conversion

As an alternative to condominium ownership, apartments may also be developed for, or converted to, cooperative ownership. A cooperative is created by a stock corporation, which holds title to the building and issues an authorized number of shares of stock to tenant-shareholders at a specified par value. The price per unit determines the number of cooperative shares a co-op member must purchase to acquire a *proprietary lease* to his or her unit. Under the lease, the tenant-shareholder makes a monthly payment to cover a pro rata share of operating expenses and debt service. Compared with condominium owners, cooperative purchasers are likely to encounter greater restrictions when negotiating the purchase of cooperative shares, financing[6] the purchase of such shares, and using the apartment unit, but fewer disagreements regarding the operation of the building, which the co-op corporation oversees. Nationwide, there are an estimated 750,000 housing units under cooperative ownership.

---

6. Developers take out master loans to cover the costs of conversion. To finance the purchase of the shares to their individual units, tenants secure end loans, often from the same lender who has underwritten the developer. Alternatively, the developer may help finance the cooperative purchaser by taking back a second mortgage on the buyer's leased premises and holding the buyer's cooperative stock as collateral until the debt is repaid. Cooperative markets are both upscale and moderately priced. In New York City, for example, there have long been luxury cooperatives. Forty-year co-op mortgages have been available from the FHA since 1951 and from HUD since 1963. The National Co-op Bank, created by Congress in 1978, finances co-op conversions of subsidized multifamily housing. See Eleanor Gunn and John Simpson, *Cooperative Apartment Appraisal* (Chicago: Appraisal Institute, 1997).

CHAPTER 4

Income Capitalization Approach

Introduction

The principal motivation to own or invest in apartment properties is to derive the income from the rents and the revenue from services or facilities provided for the tenants. The specific focus of the income analysis is the property's net operating income, or the income remaining after vacancy and collection losses and total operating expenses have been deducted from gross income. The income capitalization approach is based on the principle of anticipation, which states that value is created by the expectation of benefits to be derived in the future. In other words, the value of an apartment property reflects what a prudent purchaser-investor would pay for the present worth of an anticipated annual income stream and the reversionary benefit to be realized at the end of the anticipated holding period.

The appraisal of apartment properties mirrors the market's perception of the risks associated with ownership. Such risks include

- Vacancies, collection expenses, and evictions

- The possibility of increased municipal assessments or decreased municipal services

A body of water, either natural or man-made, is a common amenity of large garden apartment communities. Photograph of Promontory Point in Newport Beach, California, courtesy of Irvine Apartment Communities.

- The prospect of rent controls

- The loss of locational desirability

- Damage wrought by storms, fires, or other disasters

These risks can be mitigated by a variety of means, including effective property management, public relations, property insurance, and efficient rehabilitation and modernization programs.

In addition, there is the capital risk associated with liquidating the investment, either entirely, through sale, or partially, through mortgaging to another party or entity. This risk is directly tied to the perceived rentability of the property at the time of liquidation. The difference between the owner's equity at the time of liquidation and the owner's initial and subsequent investment translates into the capital gain or loss for the investment. This capital gain or loss is distinct from net operating income or operating losses during the investment period. The acquisition of an apartment property, therefore, provides an opportunity for gain or loss on both the capital invested and the ongoing operation.

Like other types of improved real estate, apartment buildings are also wasting assets. Their economic lives can be extended by general maintenance and through repair and replacement of components. Such maintenance and rehabilitation expenditures, however, are funded from what would otherwise be additional net income to the building. These expenditures can be considered either directly among the operating expense items (as variable expenses) or indirectly as capital reduction items (i.e., replacement reserves or borrowed capital).

The methods available for capitalizing income differ in respect to three features:

1. The timing of income

2. The expenses and allowances that are deducted from the income being capitalized

3. The apportionment of income among physical, financial, or ownership interests that may occur either before or after capitalization

For direct capitalization, the timing of income is generally within a 12-month period. Depending on the nature of the appraisal, however, this period may be the 12 months preceding the effective appraisal date (sometimes the basis for property assessment), the 12 months after the effective appraisal date, or some other variation, such as 12 times the operating experience of the month in which the effective appraisal date falls. The selection of the capitalization rate will vary with the period of the income to be capitalized. In discounted cash flow analysis, the income stream is forecast over a longer term, which often runs 10 years or more.

An appraiser can use several means to disaggregate property income. Potential gross income is the total of management-assigned rent for each apartment in the property. Other or miscellaneous income is also considered a component of potential gross income. The deduction of vacancy and collection losses from potential gross income results in effective gross income, sometimes called *collected gross income*. In one form of capitalization, the appraiser applies relevant multipliers to these income streams, that is, a potential gross income multiplier (*PGIM*) or effective gross income multiplier (*EGIM*). From effective gross income, an estimate of expense items is deducted to arrive at an indication of the net operating income (*NOI*). Generally, this is the income stream that is converted into value by application of a capitalization rate or discount factor. In a further refinement of *NOI*, anticipated capital expenditures in the form of a replacement allowance or reserve are deducted either on an average annual basis, as in direct capitalization, or on an anticipated actual basis, as in multiyear forecasts made in discounted cash flow analysis.

Another way to apportion property income is among physical, financial, or ownership components, i.e., land and building, mortgage and equity, or leased fee and leasehold interest (for example, the holder of a ground lease and the ground tenant). Residual techniques for analyzing the value of these components are applied before the apportioned income is capitalized. Alternatively, overall income can be capitalized into an indication of total property value to be subsequently apportioned among specific interests.

Estimating and Analyzing Income
Market Rent and Contract Rent

In the income capitalization approach, the appraiser arrives at an estimate of market rent, or rental income the subject property would likely command in the open market, by analyzing current rents paid and asked for space in comparable buildings.[1] Estimated market rent is important for both proposed and operating properties. In the case of the former, market rent allows the forecast of gross income, and with the latter it is used to calculate the income for vacant rental space or space occupied by the ownership or property management. Contract rent is the actual rental income specified in a lease. It is calculated for operating properties from existing leases, including month-to-month extensions of former leases. It is essential to specify whether the cited rent is 1) the former or existing contract rent, 2) the asking amount sought by the landlord or property manager, or 3) the market rent estimated by the appraiser.

Other or Miscellaneous Income

In addition to income from apartment rents, income to the building may be generated from a variety of sources. License fees are paid for temporary, nonexclusive use of special facilities, such as party room or swimming pool fees. Service fees are charged for elective maid service. An apartment project may earn concession income from coin telephones, vending machines, and laundry room equipment.

---

1. In rare situations, the appraiser is justified in estimating market rent as a function of development cost or sale price of the subject property. These situations involve specially designed turnkey projects, amortizing leases, and lease-purchase transactions.

Rental income can also be generated from non-apartment space such as an on-site retail store, restaurant, beauty parlor, or physician's office. A parking garage may be leased to an operator or, alternatively, the building may directly license the parking spaces to tenants or nontenants (on-site parking, however, is often available to tenants at no additional charge). Finally, interest income may accrue on the balance between rents collected in advance and expenses paid in arrears. Interest can also be earned on security deposits, although in some jurisdictions such interest must ultimately be paid back to the tenants. Thus, other income includes rent for non-apartment space and miscellaneous income from various tenant charges.

In many instances, a significant degree of the apartment project's income stream is imputable to intangible as well as tangible personalty. Apartment properties may earn business income from profits on the rental of in-suite furniture to tenants, marking up the cost of electricity privately metered to tenants, as well as for opening tenants' doors when the key is left inside, licensing the concierge function and the coin machines, profit centers such as storage rooms (including the sale of abandoned tenant goods), and the interest on company bank accounts. (See the discussion of value allocation in Chapter 7.)

Units of Comparison

Rent is generally quoted in terms of square feet of net rentable area (NRA) or net leasable area (NLA). In some markets, net rentable area is also called *net usable* or *net occupiable area*. Net rentable area is measured from the inside surfaces of an apartment's demising walls, i.e., the walls that separate the areas leased by the tenants from one another. In other words, the net rentable area of any individual unit is the area used exclusively by that tenant. The total rent of the entire apartment building may be quoted as rent per square foot of net rentable area, rent per square foot of gross building area, rent per square foot of gross finished area, rent per apartment unit, and rent per room. Comparison of the various rental units will reveal the extent to which market tenants differentiate among units on the basis of large and small rooms, additional bedrooms, or other such features.

Income Analysis

In income capitalization, an estimate is made of the market rent that the subject property would command in the open market as of the date specified in the appraisal. In the majority of situations, the estimate of market rent is expressed as total rent per square foot of the unit of comparison rather than in components, such as minimum base rent per square foot of the unit of comparison plus surcharges or pass-through expenses, e.g., utility charges. The appraiser arrives at this estimate by analyzing the rents and occupancy levels of comparable properties. Once the comparable rents have been reduced to the same unit basis applied to the subject property, they can be adjusted in the same manner as transaction prices are adjusted in sales comparison.[2] The elements of comparison account for the reasons, justifica-

---

2. Although it is possible to estimate market rent on the basis of the rate of return to the rented asset, market rent is not generally estimated in this way.

tion, or rationale for the amount of rent paid to a comparable—e.g., the rent would have been more or less but for the apartment's small/large size or poor/good location. The elements of comparison fall under the following four categories:

1. Conditions in the lease

2. Date of the lease

3. Location of the apartment

4. Property characteristics

Special conditions stipulated in the lease are frequently attributed to differences in motivation. Non-arm's-length lease terms often reflect subjective reasons or relationships among the parties. Lease renewals or extensions negotiated with existing tenants should be especially scrutinized. For example, the building management may be willing to offer existing tenants lower rent to avoid vacancies and the expense of obtaining new tenants. Only when lease provisions are similar can rents be truly comparable. Adjustments are commonly made in situations involving whether or not the landlord pays for utilities or whether or not off-street parking is provided by the lease agreement.

Differences in rent attributable to the passage of time may reflect changes in the purchasing power of the currency or the relationship between supply and demand. Annual adjustments to apartment rents are not necessarily tied to the rate of growth in the CPI. Apartment properties sometimes experience seasonal fluctuations in market conditions, especially where leases turn over once a year. The rental data analyzed may thus reflect a seasonal peak or trough.

Differences in the location or the physical characteristics of the properties also account for differences in rent. Tenants prefer a secure, convenient location. Access to public transportation and good linkages to workplaces and retail centers are important factors in most rental markets. Among the physical characteristics to consider are the size of the individual units, the quality and condition of the building, and the availability of amenities. The level of building maintenance often reflects the quality of the property management.

In developing adjustments to comparable rents, the appraiser can also analyze benchmark data in market research reports. For example, the Institute of Real Estate Management (IREM) publishes annual reports including national, regional, and metropolitan data on median gross potential income (*GPI*), gross potential rent per square foot of rentable area, and median rent per unit for four categories of apartment buildings (elevator, low-rise with over 24 units, low-rise with 12-24 units, and garden). IREM's reports also include data on median other or miscellaneous income per square foot of rentable area and other income as a percentage of gross potential income. In addition, the Urban Land Institute, National Apartment Association, and the Multifamily Housing Institute jointly publish a survey of income and expenses for apartment properties entitled *Dollars and Cents of Multifamily Housing*. Benchmark data are often cited in the appraisal report, and the rents collected for the subject and comparable apartment properties are then compared and analyzed against such data.

Disaggregation of Income

Potential gross income, the broadest possible category of income, is variously defined as the total of management-assigned rent for each apartment in the property or as the total income attributable to the property at full occupancy before vacancy and operating expenses are deducted. Other or miscellaneous income is also considered a component of potential gross income. Scheduled rent is that portion of gross potential income derived from rent stipulated in the leases in effect on the date of the appraisal. In other words, scheduled rent is the total of the contract rents for the leased apartments and the asking rents for unleased apartments. Effective gross rent, sometimes called *collected rent,* is the total of rents anticipated or actually collected.[3] Effective gross rent excludes scheduled rent from vacant apartments and delinquent rent from occupied apartments. Effective gross rent is measured in dollars and is also expressed as a percentage of scheduled rent. The deduction for rent loss attributable to vacancy or bad debt is supported through an analysis of the recent collection history of the subject property, the vacancy rates of competitive properties, and market vacancy rates. The percentage of effective gross rent to scheduled rent may be used to measure the effectiveness of the property's leasing program and rent collection.

Effective rent, another important analytical tool available to appraisers, is the total of rents stipulated in leases, less rental concessions such as leasing incentives. Effective rent is especially useful in analyzing office buildings, but it can also be calculated for apartments when such leasing incentives are offered.

Because the operating statements for comparable properties vary with regard to specific line items, the operating statements for the subject and comparable properties should be recast to ensure consistency and provide an accurate basis for comparison.

Capitalization by Means of Income Multipliers

In the appraisal of small apartment buildings, the application of gross income multipliers is the most prevalent capitalization technique. Typically, the owner of a small apartment property occupies one unit and personally manages and maintains the building. This factor often accounts for an uneven pattern of net income from property to property and explains why an appraiser may have to rely on gross income data. A gross income multiplier (*GIM*) is the price (or value) of the property divided by its gross income. The calculation is generally taken to two decimal places. For example, a building that recently sold for $727,500 and generates a gross income of $125,000 would have a *GIM* of 5.82.

---

3. Accounting usage and appraisal usage sometimes overlap and may not exactly correspond. For example, accountants use the term *experienced rent* as the rents tenants were actually obligated to pay. While the term might seem to suggest *collected rent,* its meaning more closely corresponds to *scheduled rent* in appraisal usage. Experienced rent may be identified on an accountant's operating statement as potential income, and collected rent as gross income. Accountants sometimes include deductions for penalties for late payment or expenses associated with efforts to collect rents in arrears within collected rent; alternatively, they at times show these deductions as separate line items.

A gross income multiplier may be developed on the basis of either potential gross income or effective gross income. The appraiser's choice of income multiplier to develop will depend on the availability and quality of gross income data. If the vacancy rate for one or more comparables is unknown or if the vacancy rate for a property seems to be unusual or atypical, a potential gross income multiplier (*PGIM*) will be developed and applied to the potential gross income of the subject property. When potential and effective gross income data are available and reliable, most appraisers will calculate both multipliers and consider both of the value indications derived.

Capitalization by gross income multipliers need not be restricted to small apartment properties. Appraisers routinely develop gross income multipliers when reporting comparable sales as well as for use as units of comparison in reconciliation.

In developing a gross income multiplier, an appraiser does not generally make adjustments to the comparable prices or rents. The transactions providing comparable gross income multiplier data must be reasonably similar and typically should not require adjustment. The multiplier itself represents a synthesis. For example, the multiplier developed from a comparable in a location inferior to that of the subject will generate lower rent and sell for a lower price. The multiplier itself is unaffected.

Adjustments to elements of the *GIM* formula, however, are justified in special circumstances. For example, the inclusion in an apartment house sale of an adjacent developable lot would likely increase the selling price without affecting the rent. Seller-provided mortgage financing, likewise, would probably increase the price of the sale comparable but not the rent. Adjustments to the comparable sale data in these cases would therefore be defensible.

The appraiser must also consider the components of the income to different comparables. Two identical apartment buildings that generate identical net incomes and have identical market values might nevertheless rent for different amounts if one landlord requires tenants to pay directly for tenant-consumed electricity and the other landlord includes this expense in the rent. Under these circumstances, both sets of potential and effective gross income multipliers derived from the properties would differ.

Analyzing Expenses

To develop an estimate of the net operating income, the appraiser analyzes expense data for the property. Net operating income (*NOI*), the income remaining after total expenses have been deducted from effective gross income, may be calculated before or after deducting replacement reserves. The actual expenses a landlord is required to defray include two specific categories: those incurred by the property itself, such as taxes and insurance, and those resulting from the operation of the property, such as utilities and maintenance. Generally, expenses incurred by the property per se are called *fixed expenses*. Expenses tied to the operation of the property, which rise or fall with occupancy, are called *variable expenses*.

For large properties, the cost of replacing items such as heating/cooling equipment or hallway carpeting may occur regularly. Thus, an allowance for replacements is treated as a separate expense. Even for smaller apartment properties, however, mortgage lenders and property managers may require that part of net operating income be withheld as a reserve to fund the replacement of building components. Consequently, appraisers often estimate an allowance for replacements when projecting cash flow to be capitalized into market value. Other allowances are sometimes made for unusual circumstances—e.g., reserves to cover periodic non-annual repairs, eventual compliance with environmental regulations (asbestos removal), or bringing the building up to code for handicapped persons. Estimates of such reserves should be included in the income forecast if the appraiser believes the situation warrants it.

Because of possible differences in the way accountants and property managers enter line-item expenses, the appraiser should ensure the subject property's operating statement is reconstructed to provide that the expense items recorded correspond to proper appraisal practice. In the reconstruction of the operating statement 1) nonrecurring past items are not repeated, 2) any deductions taken for non-operating expenses (i.e., personal expenses) are eliminated, 3) ambiguous, repetitive, or atypical expense items are recategorized, and 4) line items are appropriately grouped to facilitate analysis.

An expense comparison should be made on a uniform or standardized basis. If most of the expense comparables include a replacement reserve, an estimate of this line item should be included in the reconstructed operating statement for the subject property. Recategorizing expense items allows the appraiser to compare the operation of the subject with the operating experience of other properties and the expense averages from benchmark data.

For example, apartment managers often record air conditioning as an expense category. In some cases, this may simply cover the cost of maintaining the equipment, while in others, it includes allocations for water, electricity, supplies (filters), and maintenance. Similarly, the category for management may reflect different items because of different ways of operating a property. Some apartment managers will contract for landscaping, snow removal, boiler maintenance, and redecoration, while others have these functions performed by on-site employees. By grouping all expense items that are management-controllable, the appraiser will be able to compare the operations of buildings maintained on contract accounts with those of buildings that employ a permanent work force to look after maintenance.

Utility expenses often differ among properties because some managers operate apartments on a "self-contained" basis, whereby tenants pay directly for meterable natural gas and electricity, while other managers pay the costs of fuel for heating and cooking but not for electricity. Typically, the landlord absorbs all utility charges incurred by vacant units and public spaces (corridors, lobbies, office, basement storage rooms, laundry, parking, and exterior lighting) as well as water and sewer charges.

In analyzing operating expenses, the appraiser may also consult benchmark data. For example, the Institute of Real Estate Management's annual reports include the following expense groupings:

- Administration and management

- Utilities

- Repairs and maintenance

- Real estate taxes and insurance

- Payroll (salaries for maintenance and administrative staff)

These data are quoted per square foot of rentable area, as dollars per unit, and as percentage of effective gross income. Such data may be compared against the historic expense data for the subject and cited in the appraisal report. An array of benchmark data appears on the following page in Table 4.1, Typical Reporting of an Apartment Sale.

Units and Elements of Comparison

Expense analysis typically employs the same physical units of comparison used to estimate rents. Each line item can be estimated as a percentage of effective gross income (EGI), and the total of all expenses is then usually converted into a percentage of EGI. This percentage is known as the *operating expense ratio* (OER). The ratio of net operating income to effective gross income, the *net income ratio* (NIR), is the complement of the OER. These ratios tend to fall within specific ranges for each category of apartment properties. The appraiser considers how reasonable the OER and NIR are in comparison with past OER and NIR data for the property and comparable properties as well as regional/metropolitan OER and NIR data for the property category in IREM and other reports.

Direct Capitalization

Most apartment appraisers as well as buyers, sellers, and lenders prefer value estimates derived from direct capitalization rather than discounted cash flow analysis. Other than in cases where the client and appraiser believe that the achievable income from an apartment property has not approximated its stabilized income, the net operating income to the property can be directly capitalized as of the effective date of the appraisal, based on the current yield to the property. In this situation, the discounting of forecast cash flows on a yield-to-maturity basis is considered superfluous. The use of discounted cash flow analysis under other circumstances is discussed in the following section.

An overall capitalization rate (R_0) is the usual expression of the relationship between the net operating income and the value of the property (the R_0 is the reciprocal of a net income multiplier). Overall capitalization rates are derived from the simple formula

$$\text{Rate} = \text{Income/Value or } R_0 = I/V$$

A capitalization rate is typically expressed as a percentage. For example, if the net operating income to a comparable property were $1.8 million and its value/price were $20

Table 4.1 Typical Reporting of Apartment Sale*

Map Number 4

Name:	The Gwynn Park
Address:	1930 Prince George's Street
Legal:	Lot 6, Brandywine's Addition to Thomas Brooks' S/D
Zoning:	Elevator Apartment (EA)
Grantor:	Henry Banker, et ux.
Grantee:	Tuckendall, Inc.
Instrument Number:	61410
Date of Deed:	March 4, 200x
Date of Record:	March 9, 200x
Price:	$4,750,000
Financing:	All cash to seller

Land Area:	44,520 sq.ft.	$/sq. ft.:	$106.69
Gross Building Area (GBA):	240,920 sq.ft.	$/GBA:	$19.72
Finished Gross Area (FGA):	212,760 sq.ft.	$/FGA:	$22.33
Net Apartment Area (NRA):	197,867 sq.ft.	$/NRA:	$24.01
Number of Apartment Units:	290	$/Apt. Unit:	$16,379
Number of Rooms:	830	$/Room:	$5,723

Potential Gross Income (PGI):	$1,534,820	PGIM:	3.09
PGI per sq. ft. NRA:	$7.76	PGI per unit:	$5,292.50
Average Monthly Rent:	$441.04	Mo. Rent/No. Units:	$0.65 per sq. ft. NRA
Vacancy Rate:	7%		
Collected Gross Income (EGI):	$1,426,080	EGIM:	3.33
EGI per sq. ft. NRA:	$7.21	EGI per unit:	$4,917.50
Operating Expenses:	$946,710 ($4.78 per sq. ft. NRA)		
% Operating Expenses of EGI (OER):	66.4%		
Net Income:	$479,370 ($2.42 per sq. ft. NRA)		

Net Ratios:

NOI/PGI:	31.23%
NOI/EGI:	33.61%
OAR:	10.10%

Benchmark Data for an Elevator Apartment[†]			
PGI/sq. ft. NRA:	$7.84	PGI/Unit:	$5,347
Vacancy Rate:	6.5%		
EGI/sq. ft. NRA:	$7.29	EGI/Unit:	$4,969
Oper. Expenses/sq. ft. NRA:	$4.69	OER:	60.7%
Net Income/sq. ft. NRA:	$2.50	OAR:	9.90%

Description: Six-story plus basement brick elevator apartment built in 1937; contains 40 efficiencies and 250 one-bedroom units. No non-apartment rentable area; no on-site parking; utilities not separately metered.

---

* Supporting documents might include photo(s), typical floor plan, recent operating statement, closing statement, rent roll, and plat or plot plan.

† Benchmark data for apartment buildings in selected metropolitan areas may be found in *Income/Expense Analsysis: Conventional Apartments* (Chicago: Institute of Real Estate Management). National rate data (i.e., discount rates, *OARs*, residual or terminal capitalization rates) may be found in quarterly reports such as "National Market Indicators" (Korpacz Real Estate Investor Survey) published in *Valuation Insights & Perspectives* (Chicago: Appraisal Institute).

million, the overall capitalization rate would be 9.0% (the reciprocal, 11.1, is the property's net income multiplier).

An overall capitalization rate incorporates many considerations, including the likelihood that property income will increase, the momentum and duration of such an increase, and the risk and timing of a possible decrease. It reflects judgments regarding the recapture of investment and property depreciation. An overall capitalization rate can be developed on the basis of the relative allocation between, or weighting of, property components (e.g., mortgage and equity), and the respective capitalization rates of both components. This procedure is known as the *band of investment technique*. The specific allocation between financial components is supported by their relative risk rating based on which component has the prior claim to payment; for example, mortgagees are paid before equity investors.

Other ways to apportion *NOI* are among the physical and ownership components of the property. When the property's *NOI*, the value of one property component, and the capitalization rates of both property components are known, a residual technique is applied to estimate the value of the property component of unknown value. The income to the property component of known value is deducted from the property's *NOI*, and the residual income attributable to the property component of unknown value is capitalized. In many cases, however, it is not necessary to apportion an overall rate or net operating income to property components.

Developing an Overall Capitalization Rate

An appraiser may develop an overall capitalization rate for the subject apartment property by

- Analysis of rates derived from comparable properties and rate averages published by real estate research firms

- The band of investment technique

- The debt coverage ratio procedure[4]

Comparables' Rates   The appraiser relying on capitalization rates derived from specific comparables or rate averages published by reporting services should be aware that such rates are derived from the relationship of price and income for the year preceding the sale. Generally, however, the income for the subject property that will be capitalized is the appraiser's forecast for the year after the effective date of the appraisal.

For example, a comparable property that recently sold for $8 million generated a net operating income of $780,000 in the preceding year. Using the data, the appraiser develops an overall capitalization rate of 9.75%, as applicable to historic income. The subject property's net operating income for the preceding year was $650,000. Because of moderate inflation, the appraiser projects the *NOI* to increase by about 3% to $670,000 ($669,500) in

---

4. Only the principal procedures are presented in this chapter. For further discussion, see Joseph H. Martin and Mark W. Sussman, "The Twelve *Rs*: An Overview of Capitalization Rate Derivation," *The Appraisal Journal* (April 1997): 149-155.

the year following the effective date of the appraisal. This anticipated income growth can be incorporated into the overall capitalization rate, as illustrated below:

$$9.75\% \times 1.03 = 10.0425\%$$

A value of $6.7 million (rounded) is indicated by capitalizing the subject's trailing year's income ($650,000) with the 9.75% capitalization rate, which was extracted using the comparable's trailing year. An alternative would be to capitalize the subject income of $669,500, as forecast using the 3% growth rate, with the 10.0425% capitalization rate. This also results in a value of $6.7 million (rounded). Finally, it would be equally correct to capitalize a rounded income for the subject of $670,000 with a rounded capitalization rate of 10%. This too equals $6.7 million.

Band of Investment   An overall capitalization rate may be developed by the band of investment technique. As applied to financial components, the technique generates the following equation:

$$R_O = (M \times R_M) + (E \times R_E)$$

where M is the ratio of mortgage value to property value

   R_M is the mortgage capitalization rate or mortgage constant

   E is the ratio of equity value to property value

   R_E is the equity capitalization rate

For example, a property is financed by a 70% loan-to-value cash-equivalent self-amortizing mortgage with an R_M of 9%.[5] The appraiser develops the R_O algebraically. Provided that an income return of 8% to the 30% equity position is competitive, an overall capitalization rate of 8.7% would be supportable.

$$R_O = (.70 \times .09) + (.30 \times .08)$$
$$R_O = (.063) + (.024) = 8.7\%$$

That the mortgage constant of .09 is greater than the .08 equity capitalization rate may appear paradoxical in light of the extra risk associated with the equity component. But it is explained by the fact that the amortizing loan is entirely a wasting asset whereas loan amortization, dollar inflation, and possible population growth all represent opportunities that might enhance the reversion, the entirety of which would accrue to the 30% equity position.

Debt Coverage Ratio   As a lending criterion, mortgage underwriters establish minimum debt coverage ratios to ensure that the borrower will be able to meet debt service even if building income declines. A debt coverage ratio (DCR) is the ratio of net operating income

---

5. The mortgage capitalization rate (R_M) is the ratio of the annual debt service to the principal amount of the mortgage loan. Given the loan term and the interest rate, the annual mortgage constant can be calculated or found in direct reduction loan factor tables. Different combinations of terms and interest rates can produce almost identical R_Ms, e.g., with monthly compounding, a 20-year 6.6% loan, a 25-year 7.7% loan, and a 30-year 8.2% loan all have R_Ms that approximate 9%.

(*NOI*) to annual debt service (I_M). In developing overall capitalization rates, mortgage underwriters also make use of the debt coverage ratio. The R_0 equation is

$$R_0 = R_M \times M \times DCR$$

Overall capitalization rates derived by means of this equation are sometimes called *in-house capitalization rates*. Lenders use these rates to check the reasonableness of overall capitalization rates developed from data on comparable properties.

Given a 70% loan-to-value mortgage with an R_M of 9% and a debt coverage ratio of 1.4, an overall capitalization rate of 8.8% is developed.

$$R_0 = .09 \times .70 \times 1.4 = .088$$

If the debt coverage ratio were lower, say 1.2, the overall capitalization rate could be as low as 7.5% and still satisfy the lender.

$$R_0 = .09 \times .70 \times 1.2 = .075$$

Sometimes a client instructs the appraiser to use the debt coverage ratio procedure to develop an overall capitalization rate and also specifies the debt coverage ratio.[6] The appraiser may determine that the defined value to be estimated is investment value since the client has effectively selected the capitalization rate. While a mortgage with a lower loan-to-value ratio would represent a safer loan, such a loan would probably also generate lower interest.

When the debt coverage ratio is less than the debt ratio (the ratio of overall value to loan value), the mortgage capitalization rate (R_M) will exceed the equity capitalization rate (R_E). For example, in a community where typical loan-to-value ratios are 75% (the reciprocal—i.e., 1.33—is the debt ratio), a client instructs an appraiser to base the value opinion on a debt coverage ratio of 1.28 (the mortgage represents 78% of overall value). The annual constant for the loan is 9.6%. Applying this information to the *DCR* formula, the appraiser develops an overall capitalization rate of 9.2% (1.28 x .096 x .75) and an equity capitalization rate of 8%—i.e., $R_E = (R_0 - [M \times R_M])/E$ or $R_E = (.092 - [.75 \times .096])/.25$. Money market participants recognize that the yield on equity should surpass that of the safer mortgage loan because the leveraged equity position stands to benefit from capital appreciation.[7]

Discounted Cash Flow (DCF) Analysis
In cases where it is impractical to rely upon the estimate of a single year's stabilized income, the appraiser forecasts and discounts anticipated income to the year in which stabilization is anticipated. Such situations occur when atypical long-term leases are in place at the time of

---

6. Lending institutions often assign loan-to-value ratios to an entire category of properties (e.g., elevator apartment buildings) without knowledge of the value of the specific properties.

7. The types of leverage and relationships among capitalization rates (R_E, R_0, and R_M) and among yield rates (Y_E, Y_0, and Y_M) are explained in *The Appraisal of Real Estate*, 11th ed., 555-556.

the appraisal, major items of deferred maintenance are present, public works projects being carried out near the property have interrupted its normal operation, or the subject apartment property is a proposed development and construction, marketing, and absorption periods have to be projected. Most appraisers who employ DCF analysis tend to do a detailed forecast of each income item, operating expense, and capital contribution (replacement item) for every year until the year in which income is anticipated to stabilize. It is important to remember that the income, expenditures, and capital contributions have not occurred, but all are estimates based on assumptions about the future operation of the property.

The macro assumptions underlying a DCF analysis are typically supported by forecasts of economists. The analysis must also be internally consistent. For example, an assumption about the annual rate of inflation in the future should be reflected in the projections of rents, expenses, and yield rates. The exit or terminal capitalization rate (R_N) applied to the reversionary value must be consistent with the expected future physical condition of the property, which in turn should be related to projected maintenance costs and capital contributions. To the extent possible, the DCF analysis should also incorporate the effect of planned construction (new supply) upon vacancy levels and the income forecast.

DCF Application

The following example, Table 4.2, is presented for purposes of illustration only. The 11-year NOI forecast is based on the following assumptions:

1. Rents, electricity, and tenant charges will increase whereas income from parking (under a long-term operating lease), interest, and miscellaneous categories will remain level.

2. Each of the expense items will increase annually.

3. Capitalization of the discounted income forecast for the 11th year ($4,860,720/.0875) will yield an accurate indication of the value of the 12th-year reversion ($55,551,081).

4. It is appropriate to apply the same discount rate (12%) to all annual income streams as well as the reversion.

5. The net income discounted occurs on the last day of each year, although rents will be paid monthly, mostly in advance, and expenses will be paid monthly, mostly in arrears, excepting real estate taxes, which will be paid semiannually.[8]

The appraiser has forecast income for the first year of the DCF analysis at a slightly higher annual figure than that experienced during the calendar year preceding the effective date of the

---

8. If the discounting had been done on a semiannual frequency, a discount rate of 12.6% would have been selected for the annual incomes to achieve a similar present value conclusion; the discount rate applied to the reversion, however, would continue to be the end-of-the-year 12.0% as consistent with the date of terminal capitalization. For a more detailed discussion, see Stephen J. Albright, Sr., "Selecting the Appropriate Frequency of Discounting," *The Appraisal Journal* (October 1997): 354-360.

Table 4.2 Discounted Cash Flow Analysis

(Name) _____ Apartments
(City) ____, (State) ____

Year	Historic Results			Projected Performance											Reversion
	20__	20__	20__	20__	20__	20__	20__	20__	20__	20__	20__	20__	20__	20__	
Potential Gross Rent	$5,200,085	$5,330,507	$5,573,956	$5,969,687	$6,253,247	$6,550,276	$6,861,414	$7,187,331	$7,528,729	$7,886,344	$8,260,945	$8,653,340	$9,064,374	$9,494,931	
Vacancy & Collection Losses (6.5%)	338,005	346,483	362,307	388,030	406,461	425,768	445,992	467,176	489,367	512,612	536,961	562,467	589,184	617,170	
Effective Gross Rent	4,862,080	4,984,024	5,211,649	5,581,657	5,846,786	6,124,508	6,415,422	6,720,155	7,039,362	7,373,732	7,723,984	8,090,873	8,475,190	8,877,761	
Other Income															
Electricity	138,354	142,603	138,616	145,547	152,824	160,466	168,489	176,913	185,759	195,047	204,799	215,039	225,791	237,081	
Parking	53,639	45,778	42,936	42,936	42,936	42,936	42,936	42,936	42,936	42,936	42,936	42,936	42,936	42,936	
Tenant Charges	43,735	51,883	59,239	59,239	62,201	65,311	68,577	72,005	75,606	79,386	83,355	87,523	91,899	96,494	
Interest	17,012	14,924	4,384	4,384	4,384	4,384	4,384	4,384	4,384	4,384	4,384	4,384	4,384	4,384	
Miscellaneous	1,790	2,529	351	351	351	351	351	351	351	351	351	351	351	351	
Effective Gross Income	$5,116,610	$5,241,741	$5,457,175	$5,834,114	$6,109,482	$6,397,956	$6,700,159	$7,016,744	$7,348,398	$7,695,836	$8,059,809	$8,441,106	$8,840,551	$9,259,007	
Payroll	335,012	364,936	390,941	410,488	431,012	452,563	475,191	498,951	523,898	550,093	577,598	606,478	636,802	668,642	
Administrative	291,514	335,755	314,433	330,155	346,663	363,996	382,196	401,305	421,371	442,439	464,561	487,789	512,179	537,788	
Utilities	645,004	651,016	673,576	707,255	742,618	779,749	818,736	859,673	902,657	947,789	995,179	1,044,938	1,097,185	1,152,044	
Service Contracts	112,796	133,104	160,756	168,794	177,234	186,095	195,400	205,170	215,429	226,200	237,510	249,386	261,855	274,948	
Maintenance	373,749	429,620	436,151	457,959	480,857	504,900	530,145	556,652	584,485	613,709	644,394	676,614	710,445	745,967	
Insurance	60,873	67,012	72,004	75,604	79,384	83,353	87,521	91,897	96,492	101,317	106,382	111,702	117,287	123,151	
Taxes	331,576	373,998	393,960	413,658	434,341	456,058	478,861	502,804	527,944	554,341	582,058	611,161	641,719	673,805	
Replacements (2.5%)				139,541	146,169	153,112	160,385	168,003	175,984	184,343	193,099	202,271	211,879	221,943	
Total Expenses	$2,150,524	$2,355,441	$2,441,821	$2,703,454	$2,838,278	$2,979,826	$3,128,435	$3,284,456	$3,448,258	$3,620,231	$3,800,782	$3,990,338	$4,189,350	$4,398,287	
Net Operating Income	$2,966,086	$2,886,300	$3,015,354	$3,130,660	$3,271,204	$3,418,129	$3,571,724	$3,732,289	$3,900,139	$4,075,604	$4,259,027	$4,450,768	$4,651,201	$4,860,720	$55,551,081
Discount Factor				0.892857	0.797194	0.711780	0.635518	0.567427	0.506631	0.452349	0.403883	0.360610	0.321973	0.287476	0.287476
Discounted				$2,795,232	$2,607,784	$2,432,957	$2,269,895	$2,117,801	$1,975,932	$1,843,596	$1,720,150	$1,604,992	$1,497,562	$1,397,341	$15,969,608

(continued on next page)

Table 4.2 Discounted Cash Flow Analysis (continued)

Operating Performance

Expenses/Unit/Month	$312	$342	$355	$392	$412	$433	$454	$477	$501	$526	$552	$579	$608	$639
Income/Unit/Month	$743	$761	$792	$847	$887	$929	$973	$1,019	$1,067	$1,117	$1,170	$1,225	$1,283	$1,344
Expense Ratio	42.0%	44.9%	44.7%											
Units	574													

Exit Capitalization Rate:	8.75%
Discount Rate:	12.00%
Going-in Capitalization Rate:	8.20%
Inflation Rate:	5.00%
Annual Rent Escalation:	4.75%

Present Value Conclusions

Net Income	$22,263,242
Reversion	$15,969,608
Total Property	$38,232,850
Rounded	**$38,200,000**

	Number	sq. ft.	Total sq. ft.	Rent	Monthly Rent	Rent/ sq. ft.
1 BdRm/1 Bath	120	908	108,960	$775	$93,000	$0.85
1 BdRm/1 Bath/Den	60	1,070	64,200	835	50,100	0.78
1 BdRm/2 Bath/Den	60	1,085	65,100	835	50,100	0.77
2 BdRm/2 Bath	240	1,206	289,440	900	216,000	0.75
2 BdRm/2 Bath/Den	30	1,384	41,520	1,015	30,450	0.73
2 BdRm/2 Bath/Den	30	1,399	41,970	1,015	30,450	0.73
3 BdRm/2 Bath(TH*)	16	1,770	28,320	1,285	20,560	0.73
3 BdRm/2 Bath(TH)	16	1,841	29,456	1,285	20,560	0.70
3 BdRm/2 Bath(TH)	1	2,200	2,200	1,285	1,285	0.58
4 BdRm/2 Bath(TH)	1	2,200	2,200	1,285	1,285	0.58
Total	574	15,063	673,366	$ 10,515	$513,790	0.76
Potential Gross Rent					$6,165,480	
Vacancy @ 7.50%					462,411	
Effective Gross Rent					$5,703,069	

* Townhouse

appraisal. The forecast, however, for the first calendar year already commenced is less than the current annual rent roll of $6,165,480, or that amount reduced by the current rate of vacancy (the effective gross rent of $5,703,069) as shown at the bottom of the DCF analysis directly below the summary of rates and present value conclusions. For the first year of the forecast, potential gross rent is estimated at $5,969,687 and effective gross rent at $5,581,657.

The calculation of monthly rents at the bottom of the table indicates the diverse mix of units in the elevator building. The predominance of smaller units generating higher square foot rents should be noted. For apartments in this building, rent per square foot of livable area is inversely proportional to the amount of livable area. Because of the traditional increase in occupancy just before the beginning of the fall semester at the nearby college, which will occur three months hence, a 6.5% deduction was made for vacancy and collection losses, a percentage point lower than at present but equal to the experience of the past three years. The appraiser has selected 4.75% as the average annual rate of rental increase. The choice of a rental increase rate that is lower than the assumed annual inflation rate of 5% recognizes that the apartment building is a wasting asset. Expenses are projected at the expected rate of inflation.

The exit or terminal capitalization rate (R_N) selected, 8.75%, is higher than the going-in capitalization rate (R_0) of 8.2% (obtainable by dividing the first year's NOI of $3,130,660 by the $38,200,000 value concluded for the property). This is because the building will be 12 years older at the end of the DCF forecast. In the forecast, only a modest replacement allowance is included to cover the annual cost of new refrigerators, carpeting, and other components. Some replacement items may also be absorbed under the costs of maintenance and service contracts. However, no major capital infusion on renovation has been anticipated.

Growth Rate in Property Value

The following equation can be used to estimate the average rate of growth in property value:

$$CR = Y_0 - R_0$$

where CR is the compound rate of change in property value

Y_0 is the anticipated rate of yield to maturity, in this application equivalent to the discount rate selected

R_0 is the going-in capitalization rate

$$CR = 12\% - 8.2\% = 3.8\%$$

The 3.8% growth rate is significantly less than the assumed 5.0% rate of inflation. The 3.8% growth rate incorporates both the anticipated 4.5% annual rate of increase in NOI (reflecting the 4.75% annual increase in rents and 5.0% annual increase in expenses) and the erosion of capital indicated by the differential between the going-in capitalization rate of 8.2% and the exit capitalization rate of 8.75%. If a large capital expenditure had been anticipated during the forecast period, a higher reversionary value might have been estimated and a lower exit capitalization rate selected.

A major consideration in the estimated growth rate in property value is the expected rate of inflation. When the rate of inflation is low, as it was in the early 1960s, the compound rate of change *(CR)* indicated by the $Y_0 - R_0$ formula tends to be negative in recognition of the depreciation incurred by a wasting asset. Other factors to be considered in comparing discount and capitalization rates are the length of the period over which the income is discounted and the pattern of payments, that is, income streams changing in a regular or irregular manner. An unusual pattern of income may result from an externality, such as when a major employer relocates to a community and demand for apartments in the appraised property increases 10% annually over the next five years, but because of zoning regulations, available supply is unable to keep pace. Another situation might involve the gradual revocation of rent controls applying to a small township that is surrounded by communities with no rent control ordinances.

CHAPTER 5

Sales Comparison Approach

Introduction

Two principal reasons account for the great usefulness of the sales comparison approach. First, when a considerable degree of similarity characterizes the subject and comparable apartment properties, the indication derived will directly reflect the value perceptions of market participants. Second, when the subject and comparables are less similar or other approaches better simulate market thinking, a sales comparison analysis reveals market preferences and helps support the appraiser's conclusion of market value. While market participants usually prefer the sales comparison approach in valuations of small apartment projects, the ready comprehensibility of the approach among lay people and real estate professionals explains its equally widespread application in the valuation of larger apartment properties.

While both the cost and income capitalization approaches to value also employ comparative analysis and a broad array of market data, the specific focus of the sales comparison approach is information on closed or settled sales. A variety of ancillary transactional data—e.g., bona fide offers to purchase, refusals of offers, option and purchase contracts, sale-similar leases/long-term leaseholds, and, under certain conditions, asking-price listings—can

Market areas for luxury apartment properties tend to be larger than those for more moderate-priced apartments. Photograph of The Villas of Renaissance in San Diego courtesy of Irvine Apartment Communities.

also be analyzed. If enough reliable information is available, the sales comparison approach is as effective as either of the other approaches. Critics argue that the past or historic data analyzed in sales comparison lag behind the market, but this charge applies equally to comparable data used in the income capitalization and cost approaches.

Four economic principles guide an appraiser in applying the sales comparison approach.

1. The prices of properties tend to be established by the principle of supply and demand.

2. Sufficiently similar properties provide buyers with alternatives, which exemplifies the working of the principle of substitution.

3. The principle of balance governs the mix of the agents of production involved in creating a property as well as the pattern of land use in a neighborhood or district.

4. Externalities are evident in the effects of location and market fluctuations upon the enhancement or diminution of property value.

Overview of the Procedure

The first step in applying the sales comparison approach is to identify the real estate and property rights to be appraised and specify the defined value, the effective date of the appraisal, and any self-imposed or client-imposed limitations upon the valuation. The appraiser inspects the subject property and its neighborhood, gathering general information about the market as well as specific data about the property and competitive properties. This lets the appraiser determine the locational boundaries and time period for transactional data. (See Chapters 2 and 3.)

Sometimes, when the comparable sale properties selected are very similar, the sale prices can be analyzed directly on an entire property basis. Whether the apartment properties are similar or dissimilar, the prices of the comparables are reduced to common denominators known as *units of comparison,* e.g., price per square foot of net rentable area, price per apartment unit, or price per room. Various characteristics of each comparable sale property are analyzed to determine its degree of similarity or dissimilarity with the subject property. These characteristics are known as *elements of comparison.* Adjustments for significant differences between the subject and comparable are then applied to the comparable sale; adjustments may be made on either a whole price or a unit price basis. In the final step, the appraiser considers the reasonableness of the value conclusion indicated by the adjusted comparables.

Data Selection

The area in which an appraiser researches comparable sale properties is the same as that in which typical buyers and investors would consider purchasing alternative properties. In other words, the property's market area is where transactional data on competitive buildings are gathered. When sales of closely comparable properties are abundant, the most relevant transactions can be selected from an area smaller than the property's total market area. For example, when appraising the market value of a 24-unit building in a neighborhood of several dozen such buildings, the appraiser may use data from the subject's immediate vicinity and restrict the selection to those properties most similar to the subject.

Comparable properties, however, can be spread out over a broad area, such as garden apartments located along the suburban periphery of a metropolitan area. These projects command only modest rents, yet are closely competitive with one another. If there is insufficient transactional information on such properties in the subject's immediate neighborhood to support a value conclusion, it is necessary to gather data from a broader area. Generally, the market areas for high-rent apartments, outfitted with luxurious accommodations and many rooms, tend to be larger than the market areas for more modest properties.

Additionally, the date of the sale transaction is an important criterion for selecting comparable data. Usually, the most recent transactions or those closest to the effective appraisal date are the best indicators of market conditions at the time of the appraisal. In cases involving appraisals of retrospective or historic value, comparable sales data not knowable at the time of the appraisal are ordinarily excluded.[1]

A client may also instruct an appraiser to analyze specific categories of properties, such as sales that occurred within the last six months, current listings of similar properties, sales within the same school district as the subject, or sales for which mortgage financing was not federally insured. In such situations, the appraiser should either consider such instructions as non-exclusionary (i.e., as not limiting the inclusion of the most valid comparables) or, if that is not contractually practical, make a full disclosure that the resulting work qualifies as a limited appraisal governed by the Departure Provision of the Uniform Standards of Professional Appraisal Practice (USPAP).[2]

Appraisers use different principles to guide them in selecting comparable transactions. For example, some contend that if the comparables selected are to be truly representative, the appraiser must consider all buildings of a given category (elevator apartments constructed between 1980 and 1990), located in the community (a county), that have been sold within the past year. However, the best comparables are those that 1) are physically most similar to the subject, 2) are located nearest the subject, and 3) have sold closest to the time of the appraisal. It may be impossible to find comparables that meet all three criteria. In this situation some appraisers extend the analysis to include the sale of a property located adjacent to the subject and that of a prime competitor of the subject, even if the transactions occurred two or three years ago. Still other appraisers, seeking to contain the costs of excessive research, carry on the data analysis until a clear pattern of unit price emerges from

---

1. The appraiser might, however, consult data on transactions occurring after the effective date of the appraisal for several reasons, such as to support an adjustment to a sale price as of the effective date of the appraisal, to demonstrate the reasonableness of a trend observed at the time of the appraisal, to heed the professional advice of an advocate, or to comply with a mandatory court ruling.

2. The Departure Provision of the 1998 edition of USPAP specifies the circumstances under which "an appraiser may enter into an agreement to perform an assignment that calls for something less than, or different from, the work that would otherwise be required by the specific guidelines."

the most reliable comparables. In any of these instances, however, if the appraiser questions whether more transactional data are needed, the answer will most likely be yes.

Transactional data on the subject property also provide insight into the property's value. These data include past sales of the property, current offers to purchase and refusals of such offers, listings to sell, negotiations to acquire or create a long-term leasehold, prospective plans to subdivide or rehabilitate, and possible lawsuits, either threatened, filed, or settled. Where such information is available on the comparable properties, it too can be extremely useful.

While the focus of sales comparison is upon analysis of transactional data, the appraiser will also consider any other information that sheds light on the determination of market value. Examples include apparent compliance with fire safety regulations, suitability for disabled persons, recent detection or abatement of environmental hazards, proposed or in-progress public works nearby, or an occurrence that has stigmatized the property.

Data Sources

Obtaining accurate transactional information is generally not an easy task. The information sought by appraisers not only includes the facts of a transaction but also the subjective motivations of the parties involved. While only the parties themselves are likely to know their motivations, human reticence and conventional business practices often inhibit the parties from divulging the specific details. Interviews with the parties to a transaction are useful, although individual recollections of negotiations also tend to be imperfect. Transactional data can be found in a variety of documents the appraiser will review.

Closing Statement

Foremost among the documentary evidence is the closing statement, which may have been prepared by the settlement clerk, closing attorney, or title abstractor. A closing statement identifies the real estate, the settlement or closing date, the parties to the transaction, the costs of the transaction (agents' commissions and recording fees), and the price (how it was paid and how it was adjusted for on-premises supplies, prepaid taxes, and tenants' deposits). The closing statement is based on representations of the parties, including the written purchase-sale contract.

Purchase-Sale Contract

The contract for the purchase and sale of the property identifies the parties to the transaction, the real estate, the property interest conveyed, the price, and the date on which a meeting of the minds occurred between the parties. Sometimes, initialed changes in the text indicate a history of the negotiations. The contract also discloses obligations to which the parties agreed and which presumably influenced the price established.

Deed

A document almost always available to the appraiser, the deed represents the defensible proclamation that property ownership has changed. It serves notice to all, including the appraiser, that a transaction has occurred. The date of the deed is the date that title passed from seller to buyer. It identifies the real estate, the property rights conveyed, and the buyer and seller. Deeds are kept among the permanent records of the community.

Apartment properties, like other real estate investments, are often held by partnerships created for the sole purpose of owning single properties. Sometimes a deed will simply identify the seller and buyer of an apartment complex, for example, the Wild Acres garden apartments, by the initials of the partnerships, Wild Acres J.V. (joint venture) and Wild Acres L.P. (limited partnership). Usually, however, the name of the principal of both parties will be indicated. In most jurisdictions, deeds do not reveal the price paid and received and are unlikely to disclose other conditions regarding the transaction.

Deeds are usually recorded at the local courthouse within one or two business days after the passing of title at the settlement or closing. Most jurisdictions impose a fee or tax on the recording of documents as permanent records, and often for deeds, the tax is a function of the price alleged by the person presenting the deed to the clerk. However, transactions between otherwise tax-exempt entities and between family members may be exempt from this fee. If a buyer assumes a preexisting mortgage, jurisdictions sometimes waive the fee on the technicality that the recording of the transaction has already been taxed. In other jurisdictions, the fee on the recording is based on the number of pages being recorded rather than the alleged price.

When there is a tax based on the alleged price, market participants and appraisers often infer the price from the amount of tax that was paid for the recording. The tax is public information and in many jurisdictions is actually noted on the face of the deed. In jurisdictions that require both the buyer and seller to attest to the recorded price, the local recording tax is generally considered a reliable indication of the settled price. If the recording clerk accepts the representation of the purchaser alone, the recorded price may exceed the actual price. The payment of a higher fee than owed is generally not prohibited. The additional amount paid on an inflated price may be low in relation to the potential advantage gained by the purchaser from public notice that a higher-than-actual price was paid for the property.

Some government entities and corporations make it a matter of institutional policy to reveal actual prices in deeds resulting from transactions to which they are parties. A few states require that recorded deeds reveal the precise amount paid for the property acquired. In the counties of other states, local compliance is often optional. Jurisdictions that do not require recorded deeds to specify actual transaction prices perhaps unwittingly abet the dissemination of disinformation and obscure useful knowledge that would add stability to the real estate and mortgage markets. Shrouding in privacy the prices paid for real estate serves no public purpose, any more than would keeping secret the prices paid for listed securities.

Other Sources

Among comparable data, an accountant's notes to the property owner's balance sheet generally represent a credible document, providing information such as the date acquired and the price paid. Other available sources that may not be uniformly reliable include mortgage applications, publicity releases, and newspaper interviews.

Sometimes the appraiser cannot establish the price paid on the basis of documents, either because of an omission of such information in the deed/recording or the unavailability of the closing statement and purchase-sale contract. In these situations, it may be possible to glean information on the price, terms, and conditions of the comparable sale by interviewing parties who have access to the closing statement or contract. Such persons may be the sales agent, the legal representatives of the parties, the purchaser's mortgage lender, or possibly one or both of the parties. Just as an appraiser may delegate the interviewing task to another, the primary source for transactional information may also refer subsequent inquiries to the appraiser to whom such information has previously been revealed.

An appraiser will be justified in conducting more than one interview to verify information about a comparable sale. The reasons for multiple interviews include an unclear passage in a document, contradictory press reports, confusion about the physical condition of the premises upon the date of conveyance, or the need for more information on the motivations of the parties, the financing terms, or the occupancy levels and rents at the time of the transaction.

Elements of Comparison

Elements of comparison refer both to specific characteristics of purchase-sale transactions and to particular property attributes that give rise to price differences. An appraiser employs these elements to gain insight into how the prices of the comparable apartment properties were established and in what ways those properties are similar to and different from the subject. Elements of comparison are grouped under the following four categories:

1. Motivation of the parties

2. Date of the transaction

3. Location of the apartment property

4. Property characteristics

Motivational Differences

Pressure on either of the parties arising from a special relationship and the anticipated personal, financial, or legal consequences of the transaction can reduce or enhance the price of an apartment property. For example, the prices transacted in a sale between a parent and a son or daughter, between a joint ownership and a closely held business under the control of the former owners, or between a debtor and a creditor may not represent market value. A business opportunity that prompts an owner to suddenly liquidate his position in an apartment property in order to raise funds to invest in another business venture may have depressed the price of the property. The price paid for a 20-unit apartment property by the owner of its adjacent twin, who seeks greater economies of scale in managing the two buildings, may have exceeded market value.

In many cases, the appraiser knows intuitively that a sale does not qualify as a comparable—that it does not reflect the market value of the property. Appraisers are likely to eliminate transactions motivated by considerations unrelated to the economics of the apartment property. Such motivations are alien to the definition of market value and defy rational methods of estimating adjustments.

In some circumstances, the price paid for an apartment property is affected by the mortgage financing that facilitates the acquisition of the property.[3] This occurs when that financing 1) is already in place, 2) reflects the willingness of the seller to defer receiving payment (e.g., a purchase-money mortgage), 3) was placed with a conventional mortgage lender but guaranteed or insured by a government agency, or 4) was provided directly by a government agency. Mortgage financing already in place may consist of a preexisting assumable loan or a seller-arranged mortgage in which the seller pays the purchaser's mortgagee, or lender, the charges for the points (i.e., the seller "buys down" the loan). By making the cash payment to the lender, the seller enables the buyer to obtain an advantageous loan in exchange for a higher price than would have otherwise been obtainable.

In individual cases, the appraiser may define market value as encompassing any specified financing, including financing that is not cash-equivalent if it happens to characterize the given market. For example, an appraiser is asked to estimate the market value of an apartment building encumbered with assumable, buyer-favorable debt. Because such non-cash-equivalent financing is, in fact, typical of this market, the appraiser is able to directly analyze comparable sales that have similar financing. If transactional data reflecting comparable financing arrangements are not available, the appraiser will adjust all comparable sales to reflect what the sellers would have received on an all-cash basis, whether the purchasers had borrowed conventional funds or not. The adjusted sales, which indicate the subject's market value on an all-cash basis, are then adjusted to reflect the subject financing. In every case, the appraiser must measure and report the impact of favorable or unfavorable financing.

A transaction facilitated by non-cash-equivalent financing, whether typical or not, can also be adjusted to a cash-equivalent amount and then analyzed against other elements of comparison to indicate the cash value of the appraised property. The term *cash equivalent* represents the seller's point of view. A seller may defer receiving all or part of the purchase price to accommodate a purchaser who would otherwise have to borrow from a third-party conventional lender. The financing may be for the seller's convenience—i.e., the seller may

---

3. Secured debt may be funded by municipalities, counties, and occasionally life insurance companies through bond instruments rather than mortgage or trust instruments. The terms of the loan rather than its technical designation, however, represent the element of price comparison.

prefer the purchaser's note to some other arrangement. Or, the financing may help a buyer who is unable to arrange a loan within the time, in the amount of the negotiated price, or at the lower rate proffered by the seller. Seller-provided financing reduces the expense of loan placement as well. Whether or not the seller lends the money, the purchaser is likely to borrow an amount to cover most of the price, and no loan is the true equivalent of cash to a purchaser who does not have the alternative of paying cash.

Other possible encumbrances also limit the rights obtained when title to an apartment property is transferred. When an apartment property is under a long-term lease to an institution such as a college, the appraiser would want to know if the leasehold was included in the transaction. Similarly, a comparable property may be subject to a life estate, a facade preservation easement, or the spacious grounds of the property subject to a previous transferable development rights agreement. Such encumbrances will restrict the future use and present value of the property interest sold.

Date of the Transaction

Two factors account for price differences attributable to changes over the time since the date of the comparable transaction: inflation and market conditions. Inflation is the erosion in the purchasing power of currency over time, characterized by price escalation. The federal government publishes price indices tracking the pattern of inflation for a sample "fixed market basket" of goods and services. The Consumer Price Index for All Urban Consumers, or CPI-U, compiled by the U.S. Department of Labor is the oldest and most widely consulted index in this country.

Market conditions at national, regional, and local levels influence a community's disposable income, the strength of consumer confidence, the availability and cost of mortgage money, the demand for and ultimately new supply of apartment units, and the level of real estate and nonrealty investment. Government activity can directly affect market conditions. For example, some government agencies construct or subsidize the construction of new apartments. Government policy may provide income tax advantages to landlords of apartment properties, apartment tenants, or apartment owners.

Severe market conditions can precipitate an unreasonable degree of speculative demand, which is reflected in rapidly increasing prices, usually transacted through contract sales, sometimes at intervals too short to allow sufficient time for appraisal advice. At the other extreme, adverse market conditions can create a two-tiered market; prices at one level are lower than what willing sellers would accept except under duress, and prices at the other level are higher than what the only available purchasers would pay. Such a dislocated market may be exacerbated by the absence of normal lines of mortgage credit, causing market participants inconvenience and even hardship. Sound appraisal judgment is needed to determine how changing market conditions affect market value.

In deriving an adjustment for changes over the time that has elapsed since the date of the comparable transaction, the appraiser must consider both inflation and market conditions. A net adjustment for this element of comparison is likely to be less than the corresponding rate of inflation if adverse market conditions diminish or offset the effect of inflation. On the other hand, improved market conditions may indicate a net adjustment greater than the corresponding rate of inflation. One helpful approach is to consider inflation and market conditions as distinct factors and apply separate adjustments. Paired data analysis may also be used to isolate the degree of difference in price over the time that has elapsed since the date of the comparable transaction. However, a net adjustment supported by this pairing procedure incorporates both the effect of inflation and the change in market conditions.

Location of the Apartment Property

As is true of any type of real estate, the location of an apartment property is a critical element of comparison. Location refers to a variety of features, including

- The general neighborhood in which the property is situated

- Accessibility by car both to and from the neighborhood

- Availability and adequacy of public facilities or services (transportation, schools, police, street cleaning and lighting, refuse removal)

- Compatibility with other neighborhood buildings and land uses (apartment, residential, or commercial properties) in scale, architecture, maintenance, price, and occupancy

The appraiser also considers the location of the apartment property in relation to thoroughfares preferred by neighborhood residents and the siting and accessibility of the apartment building (street/alley frontage and corner influence). Generally, rents also vary with the desirability of the view. The surrounding neighborhood forms this urban or suburban landscape. Paired data analysis is sometimes used to isolate the effect of location upon price. In other cases, the appraiser will form a judgment based on the analysis of secondary comparables or on the circumstances of previous appraisals.

Property Characteristics

Differences among properties stem from land use or zoning regulations, the type of occupancy, and the physical and functional characteristics of the buildings. The value of two otherwise competitive apartment buildings located in different jurisdictions is likely to vary if the zoning in one jurisdiction requires off-street parking while the other does not. Conversion to condominiums may be permitted in one community and prohibited in another. One jurisdiction may have rent controls but the other does not. Or one of the apartment buildings may be subject to a private deed restriction that requires maintaining the excess land at a cost higher than the additional rent generated by this amenity. Furthermore, the occupancy of highly comparable buildings may differ according to tenant turnover rate or average lease term.

The physical and functional features that account for property differences include

- Differences in materials, construction quality, and building condition

- Inadequate or out-of-date building systems (HVAC, plumbing, electrical, mechanical, security, and fire-safety)

- Layout and appeal of the buildings, grounds, common areas (corridors, lobbies), and individual units

- Other features that induce tenants or buyers to pay more or less for otherwise similar properties

The appraiser should investigate the cost-benefit relationship between the installation and maintenance of expensive outfittings and the additional rental income produced, whether or not the apartment units are equipped with individual utility meters, and the availability of facilities such as swimming pools or common rooms.

Organizing the Data

Once the comparable sales have been selected, the appraiser prepares a description of each property and associated transaction. The property description reflects the condition on the date of sale and covers the following items:

- Physical features of the land

- Building structure

- Building layout

- Building systems

- Appliances in both the individual units and common rooms

- Fixtures

- Surfaces (walls, floors, ceilings)

- Possibly personalty, such as furniture, equipment, supplies, and vehicles

Another item to note is whether the comparable property conforms to the zoning and the ramifications of any recent change in zoning on property use. The property description also includes apartment rents, services provided by the landlord, other sources of income (store or office rents and license or use fees for parking, swimming pool, and laundry), and occupancy levels. The highest and best use of each comparable is considered in terms of necessary renovation or possible subdivision or conversion.

If a comparable transaction is conditional upon the seller obtaining some permission, making a physical alteration, or providing financial assistance, the description of the transaction should specify the contract terms. This description includes the nominal price, any financing provided by the seller, any obligations of the seller, and the date of the sale.

Sometimes, it is useful to consider other dates and price information, such as when the property was first listed for sale and for how much, when the original asking price was formally reduced and by how much, or when the contract settlement and recording occurred. At other times, however, these dates and price data, which reflect ongoing negotiations between the parties, are unreliable as predictors of marketing time or price. Other items to include are the identities of the parties and any business pressures under which the sale was transacted.

Units of Comparison
Financial Units

The relationships or ratios between the price/value of a comparable property and its recent or anticipated income represent financial units of comparison. As noted in Chapter 4, the income can be compared on the basis of scheduled rent or collected rent, also called *effective gross rent*. In addition, gross income or net income streams can be compared, that is, before or after deducting actual or projected operating expenses. The income divided by the price/value results in a percentage or capitalization rate. The price/value divided by the income produces a rate-reciprocal or factor, usually referred to as a *multiplier*. Generally, two types of multipliers are compared: a monthly gross rent multiplier is the unit of comparison analyzed for single apartment units, while an annual gross rent multiplier is analyzed for apartment buildings.

In some communities, a self-contained one-bedroom apartment unit might sell for approximately 140 times a single month's rent (140 = the monthly *GRM*). The apartment buildings might sell for eight times annual scheduled rent (8 = the annual multiplier based on scheduled rent), nine times anticipated annual collected rent (9 = the annual multiplier based on collected rent), and generate a net operating income that is 10% of price (R_0 = 0.10). In developing such rates and multipliers, the appraiser may adjust either the income or the price component for differences between the comparable and subject. Both components, however, should not be adjusted in developing any one multiplier. The appraiser uses capitalization rates and income multipliers in the income capitalization approach to derive a value indication. In sales comparison, however, the appraiser considers differences between the ratios or the price and income components of such ratios and attempts to explain the reason for variance.

Physical Units

More physical units of comparison are available for analyzing apartment properties than for other property types such as office or retail buildings. Examining these units provides an understanding of room and unit size, building efficiency, and property operating costs. The analysis of physical units of comparison also facilitates the selection of sales for paired data analysis.

Physical units of comparison include the price/value per apartment unit, per apartment room, per gross square foot of building, per finished square foot of building, and per net square foot of building. In accordance with local practice, the net square footage of a building is also variously referred to as the occupiable area, livable area, or rentable area. For individual apartments, the price per apartment unit is the most common unit of comparison, followed by price per net square foot. Some appraisers also base their comparisons upon the number of bedrooms per apartment.

Physical units of comparison can only be developed when sufficient and accurate information is available from the most indicative comparable sales, i.e., those recent sales that are especially similar to the subject in location and construction. The most appropriate physical units of comparison are those that participants in the market rely on and those that shed the most light on price differences among comparable properties. Although price per unit is nearly always compared in the market, price per apartment room may be more useful when the number of rooms per apartment varies significantly among the comparables. Similarly, price per net square foot serves as an especially appropriate unit of comparison when the average number of net square feet per apartment room varies significantly among the comparables. Price per gross square foot of building area can be a useful unit of comparison when there is considerable disparity among the comparables regarding nonresidential building area that can be used for service-retail, parking, or recreation.

Apartment Count   In the apartment count for the comparable and subject properties, most appraisers include all residential units that can be rented (or sold) on the open market. This includes staff-occupied units, although occasionally a unit such as a basement apartment occupied by the janitor is not legally marketable. Apartments that are out of service are also generally included. Data on the costs associated with their repair and lease-up may be useful in deriving an adjustment to bring a comparable price into conformity with the existing condition of the subject property.

Area Measurement   The property inspection phase of an appraisal is covered in Chapter 3. However, to reiterate, *gross building area* is defined as the total floor area of a building, including below-grade space but excluding unenclosed areas, measured from the exterior surfaces of the outside walls. Sometimes, an appraiser adopts the architectural measure of gross floor area, which differs from gross building area in that shaft or atrium areas are excluded. Although the dimensions and area calculations in the drawings of a registered architect should be reliable, it is important to check that all modifications included in the architect's design were incorporated into the building. Registered architects initial and date each sheet of their drawings where any modification is made, and the drawings are stamped when the building permits are issued. Greater care is required to establish the accuracy of area calculations made by non-architects such as space planners, marketing agents, or publicists. The net area of an apartment unit is the floor area bounded by the interior surfaces of the demising walls, which include the outside wall of the building, the corridor wall, and walls of any adjacent apartment units.

Apartment Rooms   There is no universally accepted definition of *apartment room*. The room count for comparable properties should be on the same basis as that for the subject. Some clients prefer to specify what they want included in the count of apartment rooms. As long as a client's direction is applied consistently, it is permissible to accept it despite the somewhat arbitrary nature of any such definition. Otherwise, the best course of action is to accept the definition of apartment room that the community normally uses. In some communities, the number of rooms in an apartment is equated to "the number of bedrooms plus two," or "plus a dining room or den when these areas are not part of another room." Under such a formula, an efficiency or studio apartment has two rooms, and a two-bedroom-and-den apartment has five rooms.

Room Size   Differences in apartment size do not necessarily translate into differences in rent. A 700-sq.-ft. apartment can command the same rent as a 735-sq.-ft. apartment even though the latter incurs greater operating expenses. The additional 5% of floor area could result from an awkward configuration, an oversized entrance, or a larger interior hallway. An appraiser may also find an inverse relationship between the price/value per apartment room and the number of rooms in the apartment—i.e., an increase in the price per room as the number of rooms in the apartment decreases. This is consistent with the observation that specialized uses correlate with greater costs. Essential bathroom and kitchen areas are those with the highest square foot cost. Often the bathrooms and kitchens are identical in efficiency apartments and larger one-bedroom or two-bedroom units. But the additional rooms in the larger apartments have no plumbing, no cabinetry or appliances, and less expensive surfaces.

Parking Spaces   For garden apartments, it is especially useful to calculate the parking spaces per apartment and land area per apartment to determine whether the parking and open space are adequate or, in some cases, superadequate. Superadequate parking and open space result in higher maintenance and insurance expenses, and possibly higher real estate taxes, although apartment tenants are unlikely to pay anything additional for this superadequacy. As a result, a garden property with superadequate parking and open space has a lower market value per unit of comparison.

Entrances and Stairways   Some walk-up garden apartments have outside covered stairs attached to the external walls of the building. These stairways are unlikely to be included in either the gross building area or gross floor area. Other similar garden apartments have heated entrances and interior stairwells, which add to the gross building areas of those properties. If the two types of garden apartments are of the same construction, it can be assumed that the buildings with the enclosed entrances and interior stairwells will sell for a lower price per gross square foot of building area. Furthermore, if assessments are based on the gross square footage of building area, or if the tenants perceive a greater security threat from enclosed entrances, the larger building may also sell at a lower price per net square foot, per apartment, and per room.

The analysis of physical units of comparison leads to an understanding of complex relationships among building features. To some degree, excessive size and increasing operating costs must affect the valuation by reducing the gross rent multiplier applied to rent or the net income capitalized, and by adding to the functional obsolescence estimated.

The Adjustment Process

A data array grid is commonly used to organize and compare the data on the subject and comparables properties. The least appropriate comparables and associated transactions can be eliminated from the data analysis first. These will include transactions that occurred well in the past, properties that differ in location and physical characteristics from the subject, sales of property interests that differ from the interest being appraised, and transactions subject to terms and conditions that do not meet the criteria for market value. Patterns will begin to emerge from an analysis of various unit prices. At this point, a sale lying outside the pattern may also, upon verification of the data, be eliminated. Then, the appraiser focuses on the most indicative comparables to determine whether more information is needed and to consider how each comparable differs from the subject property. At this point, any required adjustments are made to the comparable sale prices for specific differences in the elements of comparison.

Generally adjustments are applied in the same sequence as that in which the elements of comparison have been discussed above. Assume for purposes of illustration that like the subject, the most indicative comparables are operating apartment houses, the property interest conveyed in each of the transactions was the fee simple, and none of the parties to any of the transactions were atypically motivated. The appraiser must consider whether the price of any comparable was affected by seller-arranged financing. If the market value definition being used specifies all cash and one of the comparable prices was affected by seller-arranged financing, the comparable price should be recalculated on an all-cash basis. One of several methods for making a financing adjustment is to compare the advantages of the seller-arranged loan with the market-available financing by means of discounting the sets of future cash flows servicing each loan. In most cases, it is reasonable to assume that the purchaser-borrower will liquidate the loan well before the 20- to 30-year life of the typical long-term mortgage.

Next, the appraiser would consider each comparable sale for any possible changes between the date of sale and the effective date of the appraisal. Thus, cash or cash-equivalent sale prices will be adjusted for inflation, to reflect the purchasing power of the dollar on the effective appraisal date, and any differences in market conditions that may have changed the demand situation. Most apartment sale/purchase transactions are not final on the contract date, or date when the parties achieve a meeting of the minds regarding the terms and price. Rather, the sale/purchase is contingent upon one or more future events, such as the purchaser obtaining a specified type and amount of financing. The contract date, therefore, is less representative of the price than is the settlement date, or date of conveyance, when the purchaser generally takes possession. Both parties to a contingent contract will have agreed to an approximate settlement date, and their negotiations over price have presumably incorporated inflation and other time-related changes they anticipate between the contract date and settlement date—changes which may or may not materialize. In most cases there is no significant difference between the settlement date and the date on which the deed is recorded.

Any differences between the subject and selected comparables now remaining are attributable to location or the physical characteristics of the properties. Adjustments for locational or physical differences are made on the basis of paired data analysis and the appraiser's judgment.

Quantitative and Qualitative Methodologies

Quantitative adjustments are applied to comparable sale prices either as dollar amounts or percentages. It may be appropriate to calculate adjustments for certain elements of comparison as dollar amounts and other adjustments as percentage amounts. For example, if a comparable apartment building is subject to a municipal rent control ordinance, the income loss can be capitalized and deducted as a dollar amount. Similarly, an adjustment for the cost of necessary repairs resulting from a fire that has damaged one of the units in an apartment building can be calculated in dollars. On the other hand, the marketplace might consider a locational advantage/disadvantage or superior/inferior physical condition on a percentage basis.

The differences between the subject and a comparable sale may also be analyzed qualitatively. In qualitative analysis, the appraiser uses relative comparison and ranking to determine which properties are inferior, superior, and more or less similar to the subject. The comparable properties are arranged in an array according to degree of comparability to the subject, and a bracket for the value of the subject is thereby indicated.[4] For example, the appraiser concludes that a highly comparable property is superior to the subject in location but slightly inferior in physical condition. Overall the comparable is deemed superior to the subject. If this property is the most similar among the other comparables that are judged superior to the subject, its price may set the upper bracket on the value of the subject.

It is also possible to combine quantitative and qualitative methods, adjusting comparable sale prices for differences that can be calculated quantitatively and then ranking the sale properties according to overall comparability with the subject.

Application

The following application illustrates an apartment property appraisal based on analysis of unit prices. After eliminating several other possible comparable sales from consideration, the appraiser applies quantitative adjustments to the unit prices of the three remaining comparables for differences in financing, market conditions/purchasing power, location, and

---

4. For an example of an apartment property appraisal based on qualitative analysis, see *The Appraisal of Real Estate*, 11th ed., 437-440.

physical condition. The appraiser then analyzes the range of unit prices indicated for the subject. Among other features, the comparable properties differ from the subject in area, number of units, and number of rooms. The data array and adjustment grids are for purposes of illustration, and the reader should not infer that these unit prices must be the only ones available or are necessarily the most indicative. Descriptive information on the subject and comparables is provided in the data array grid shown in Table 5.1.

Comparable sales 2 and 3 are larger than the subject property, and Comparable 1 is smaller. However, Comparable 3 has more finished area and more rooms than Comparable 2, although Comparable 2 has significantly more apartments. Comparable 3 has an average of 3.64 rooms and 872 finished square feet per apartment unit, which indicates that in these respects it exceeds the subject and other two comparables. But Comparable 3 has less finished area per average room than the other two comparable sales. It is not surprising, therefore, that its price per room was the lowest of the comparables while its price per apartment unit was the highest.

The three adjustment grids that follow, Tables 5.2, 5.3, and 5.4 present a comparison of possible value indications for the subject based on unit prices.

Table 5.1 Data Array Grid

	Subject	Comparable 1	Comparable 2	Comparable 3
Address	88 Rush Lane	38 Monmouth St.	10 Myrtle Ave.	4 Aquasco Dr.
Finished Area	35,373 sq. ft.	26,660 sq. ft.	56,424 sq. ft.	58,457 sq. ft.
No. of Apartments	62	46	86	67
No. of Rooms	136	106	220	244
No. of Rooms per Apartment Unit	2.20	2.30	2.56	3.64
Finished Area per Apartment Unit	570 sq. ft.	580 sq. ft.	656 sq. ft.	872 sq. ft.
Finished Area per Room	260 sq. ft.	252 sq. ft.	256 sq. ft.	240 sq. ft.
Price	—	$1,563,763	$2,500,000	$2,750,000
Price per Apartment Unit	—	$33,995	$29,070	$41,045
Price per Room	—	$14,752	$11,364	$11,270
Price per Finished Area	—	$58.66 per sq. ft.	$44.31 per sq. ft.	$47.04 per sq. ft.

Table 5.2 Adjustment Grid: Price per Square Foot of Finished Area Adjusted for Financing, Market Conditions, Location, and Condition

	Subject	Comparable 1	Comparable 2	Comparable 3
Finished Area	35,373 sq. ft.	26,660 sq. ft.	56,424 sq. ft.	58,457 sq. ft.
Price per Finished Area	—	$58.66 per sq. ft.	$44.31 per sq. ft.	$47.04 per sq. ft.
Financing/Market Conditions	—	– 20%	Similar	– 5%
All-Cash as of the Effective Date of the Appraisal	—	$46.93	$44.31	$44.69
Location	—	Similar	+ 10%	+ 5%
Price Adjusted for Location	—	$46.93	$48.74	$46.92
Physical Condition	—	+ 5%	+ 5%	+ 5%
Price Adjusted for Physical Condition	—	$49.28	$51.18	$49.27
Value per Finished Area Multiplied by Finished Sq. Ft. in Subject		x 35,373	x 35,373	x 35,373
Indicated Value for Subject		$1,743,181	$1,810,390	$1,742,828
Net Adjustment		15%	15%	5%
Gross Adjustment		25%	15%	15%

Table 5.3 Adjustment Grid: Price per Apartment Unit Adjusted for Financing, Market Conditions, Location, and Condition

	Subject	Comparable 1	Comparable 2	Comparable 3
Finished Area per Apartment Unit	570 sq. ft.	580 sq. ft.	656 sq. ft.	872 sq. ft.
Price per Apartment Unit	—	$33,995	$29,070	$41,045
Financing/Market Conditions	—	– 20%	Similar	– 5%
All-Cash as of the Effective Date of the Appraisal	—	$27,196	$29,070	$38,993
Location	—	Similar	+ 10%	+ 5%
Price Adjusted for Location	—	$27,196	$31,977	$40,943
Physical Condition	—	+ 5%	+ 5%	+ 5%
Price Adjusted for Physical Condition	—	$28,556	$33,576	$42,990
Value per Apartment Unit Multiplied by Number of Apartment Units in Subject		x 62	x 62	x 62
Indicated Value for Subject		$1,770,472	$2,081,712	$2,665,380
Net Adjustment		15%	15%	5%
Gross Adjustment		25%	15%	15%

Table 5.4 Adjustment Grid: Price per Apartment Room Adjusted for Financing, Market Conditions, Location, and Condition

	Subject	Comparable 1	Comparable 2	Comparable 3
Finished Area per Apartment Room	260 sq. ft.	252 sq. ft.	256 sq. ft.	240 sq. ft.
Price per Apartment Room	—	$14,752	$11,364	$11,270
Financing/Market Conditions	—	– 20%	Similar	– 5%
All-Cash as of the Effective Date of the Appraisal	—	$11,802	$11,364	$10,707
Location	—	Similar	+ 10%	+ 5%
Price Adjusted for Location	—	$11,802	$12,500	$11,242
Physical Condition	—	+ 5%	+ 5%	+ 5%
Price Adjusted for Physical Condition	—	$12,392	$13,125	$11,804
Value per Apartment Room Multiplied by Number of Apartment Rooms in Subject		x 136	x 136	x 136
Indicated Value for Subject		$1,685,312	$1,785,000	$1,605,344
Net Adjustment		15%	15%	5%
Gross Adjustment		25%	15%	15%

Reconciliation

Having developed nine possible indications based on three sets of adjusted price units, the appraiser must determine which specific indications should be given greater weight and which indications should be given less. As noted, Comparable 3 exceeds the subject and other comparables in average number of rooms per apartment (3.64) and finished square feet per apartment unit (872). The appraiser may believe that these factors skew the indication based on the price per apartment unit of $42,990, shown in Table 5.3, and decide to eliminate Comparable 3 from consideration. Or the appraiser may develop an adjustment for the differing apartment sizes, using paired data analysis. Such an adjustment cannot simply be made on a pro rata basis because the larger apartment areas of Comparables 2 and 3 and the greater number of rooms in Comparable 3 might contribute less to value than unit size and room number would suggest. In developing the size adjustment, the appraiser also considers economic data gained from the other two approaches to value, i.e., the available rent and development cost differentials associated with apartment buildings with a higher or lower number of rooms and with larger or smaller room sizes.

Given the indications resulting from the unit prices after adjustment for differences in unit size and room number, a conclusion of less than $1.8 million may be warranted based on the following reasoning. Comparable 1 is the most similar to the subject in total finished area, average area per apartment unit (580 square feet), and average number of rooms per unit (2.30). The value indicated by Comparable 1 for the subject in all three adjustment grids is less than $1.8 million. The appraised property is reasonably similar to Comparable 1 and Comparable 2 in average room size (252 square feet and 256 square feet). All three indications based on price per apartment room (Table 5.4) are similar to one another (and all less than $1.8 million), although average room size for the different properties varies. This observation could be significant in that the average room size of the subject exceeds that for each of the comparables. Finally, the three indications based on price per apartment room (prior to any size adjustment) suggest a lower conclusion than do the results of the other two adjustment grids.

Additional Analytical Indicators

Statistical tools such as the measures of central tendency (the mean or average, median, and mode or most frequent or typical value) are sometimes employed to help estimate a subject property's market value in sales comparison. Generally, however, there are too few data or quantifiable variates to allow any degree of statistical reliability. While the usefulness of these measures increases with the quantity of data available, their analysis may provide additional insight into the valuation problem.

Some appraisers disregard the high-end and low-end values after analyzing several comparables that show a high degree of similarity to the subject. Many appraisers also give less consideration to any comparable that requires a large gross adjustment since the greater the adjustment becomes in absolute terms, the less similar the comparable property is to the subject.

CHAPTER 6

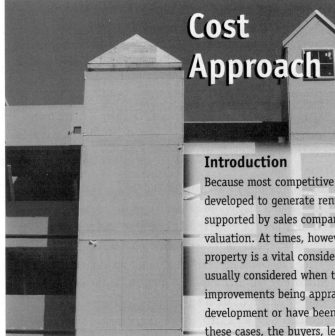

Cost Approach

Introduction

Because most competitive apartment projects are developed to generate rent, income capitalization supported by sales comparison is fundamental to their valuation. At times, however, the cost to recreate the property is a vital consideration. The cost approach is usually considered when the apartment building improvements being appraised are proposed for development or have been recently constructed. In these cases, the buyers, lenders, and prospective developers who constitute the market base their value conclusions on the cost to develop the improvements, plus land value. The cost approach is especially persuasive when the site value is well supported and the improvements are new, attractively designed, and appropriate to the site and the location. Accordingly, the improvements suffer no, or only minor, depreciation (with the possible exception of external obsolescence in the form of adverse market conditions) and thus represent the highest and best use of the site as though vacant.

A further use of the cost approach in the appraisal of apartment buildings occurs when the owner is considering structural additions or renovation. The appraiser can use this approach to determine whether the cost of rehabilitation, added apartment units, or enlarged units is recoverable through increased rental income or a higher sale price.

Development costs are more accurately estimated for new construction than for existing properties because of the difficulty in estimating depreciation.

The cost approach is especially important when the lack of market activity limits the applicability of the sales comparison or income capitalization approaches. Because reliable apartment building sales are unavailable, market indications based on a building's depreciated cost or the cost to acquire and refurbish an existing building may indeed reflect market thinking. The cost approach deserves consideration when alternative values are being estimated, such as use value or insurable value. And cost analysis can help a client decide when to develop land held for speculative purposes, that is, by comparing the present value of estimated development costs in the immediate future with the present value of estimated development costs at a more distant time.

In the case of an older apartment building with dated design and other forms of functional obsolescence, the improvement may no longer represent the highest and best use of the site. Not only is the estimation of depreciation in older buildings more difficult, but comparable information supporting the current cost to develop a replacement improvement is often lacking. For example, a mid-rise, 60-year-old, 30-unit apartment building may have undergone several renovations and upgradings. It would be extremely difficult to estimate all the requisite cost adjustments for such a building. Furthermore, in a mature, built-up neighborhood, sales of vacant land for apartment development are extremely scarce. Nevertheless, in-fill site sales may be the only basis on which the appraiser can support land value.

The cost approach is based on five economic principles.

1. Substitution affirms that no prudent buyer would pay more for a property than the cost to acquire a comparable site and build an improvement of equivalent desirability and utility without undue delay.

2. Prices fluctuate with shifts in supply and demand. Costs may not be synchronized with such changes.

3. Disequilibrium between costs and market forces affects prospective development as well as the value of existing buildings. According to the principle of balance, the agents of production (land, labor, capital, and coordination/entrepreneurship) and property components (land and improvements) must be in proper proportion for optimum property value to be achieved and sustained.[1]

4. Externalities affect the supply and demand equation, the costs of development, and purchasing power. Externalities can also take the form of an unforeseen advantage or detriment that befalls the property—e.g., improved accessibility resulting from the construction of a nearby expressway, or stigmatization caused by proximity to a site containing toxic waste.

---

1. The principle of balance as it applies to the components of a property is especially relevant in the cost approach because of the need to analyze the contributions of the site and building to property value. The cost approach affords an in-depth understanding of the mix of property components, which is essential to applying the sales comparison and income capitalization approaches.

5. The highest and best use of a site as vacant and the highest and best use of the property as improved are distinct concepts. To the extent that depreciation occurs, the existing improvements fail to reflect the highest and best use of the land, although often adding significant value to the property. When the existing improvements do not reflect the property's highest and best use, they are worthless and contribute nothing to the property's value.

While appraisers are apt to think that cost sets the upper limit on the value of an improvement, the financial sponsor or entrepreneur typically believes that the contributory value of the improvement should equal or exceed the development and marketing costs, including a reasonable profit. Thus for a sponsor, cost sets the lower limit on value. The reason for such divergent views is the time factor. The costs a developer anticipates and the costs an appraiser estimates are both based on a series of hypothetical expenditures. Even though the development and marketing of an apartment complex may span one to three years, the appraiser estimates the costs as of the effective appraisal date, either projecting current market conditions or forecasting alternative conditions that seem more probable. On the other hand, the developer willingly accepts considerable risk over the development and marketing period. This risk is associated with potential problems in the land use (zoning or engineering limitations), the construction (labor strikes, delays in deliveries, or cost overruns), the financing (interest on construction loans may be indexed to a volatile short-term money-rate), the leasing-up (stiff competition from available apartment buildings or competing construction, or a slackening in demand), and the anticipated operating expenses. Thus, it would be a remarkable developer who could subscribe to the notion that development and marketing costs, including profit, only set an upper limit on the value of the completed and operating property.

Overview of the Procedure

To apply the cost approach, the appraiser estimates the costs of building a substitute improvement for the existing structure (including an appropriate entrepreneurial profit), deducts any loss in value caused by depreciation in the existing building, and then adds the depreciated cost of the improvements to an estimate of the land value. Each estimate is as of the effective appraisal date. The procedure can be broken down into the following nine steps. The appraiser will

1. Estimate the value of the site as though vacant and available to be developed to its highest and best use. The estimate should reflect land use limitations such as zoning and easements but not financial liens such as mortgage debt or limitations upon property interests such as leases.

2. Estimate the direct (hard) and indirect (soft) costs required to develop the primary existing improvements.

3. Estimate an appropriate entrepreneurial profit from analysis of the market.

4. Add estimated direct costs, indirect costs, and the entrepreneurial profit to arrive at the total cost of the improvements.

5. Estimate the amount of depreciation in the structure and, if necessary, allocate it among the three major categories: physical deterioration, functional obsolescence, and external obsolescence.

6. Deduct the estimated depreciation from the total cost of the improvements to derive an estimate of their depreciated cost.

7. Estimate the contributory value of any site improvements or accessory buildings that have not already been considered. (Often site improvements are appraised on the basis of their contributory value, that is, directly on a depreciated-cost basis.)

8. Add the site value to the total depreciated cost of all the improvements to arrive at the indicated value of the property.

9. Adjust the indicated value of the real property for any personal property (e.g., trade fixtures, furniture, and equipment) included in the value estimate and, if necessary, adjust this value, which reflects the fee simple interest, for the property interest being appraised to arrive at the indicated value of the specified interest in the property.

Site Valuation

Sales comparison is the most commonly applied technique for appraising land under an existing or proposed apartment building. No other method is as persuasive or reliable. When sufficient sales of comparable vacant sites are not available, an appraiser may employ less direct methods such as allocation, extraction, and two other techniques that are variants of direct capitalization—land residual and ground rent capitalization.

Sales Comparison

Sales of similar land parcels suitable for development are analyzed, compared, and adjusted to provide a value indication for the subject site. After gathering data on actual sales as well as listings, offers, and purchase options, the appraiser identifies similarities and differences in the parcels, then ranks parcels according to degree of comparability with the subject. Then, with the sales arranged in a logical manner on a market data grid, the appraiser applies adjustments for differences in the comparable and the subject parcels. The final step is to reconcile the adjusted prices and form a conclusion of the most reasonable and probable market value of the subject site.

The sale parcels are analyzed by means of elements of comparison, which normally include the following:

- Property rights

- Financing terms

- Conditions of sale (motivation)

- Market conditions

- Location

- Physical characteristics

- Zoning

- Highest and best use

The most variable physical and locational characteristics relate to the size and shape of the parcel, its frontage, topography, accessibility, and view.

Units of comparison commonly applied in the valuation of land include the following:

- Price per permitted or planned apartment unit

- Price per square foot of land area

- Price per front foot

- Price per lot or parcel

- Price per square foot of allowable building area (net or gross)

- Any other unit(s) the specific market recognizes

Apartment site value is often expressed in dollars per permitted or planned apartment unit or dollars per square foot of allowable building area. In arriving at an estimate of land value, the appraiser usually correlates two or more unit prices, such as price per lot or price per square foot of land area, price per apartment unit, and price per square foot of allowable building area (net or gross).

Physical units such as price per front foot or price per square foot of land area are excellent yardsticks of the comparability of a parcel in terms of location, size/shape, topography, and orientation/view. Zoning is often the most basic criterion for selecting comparable land sales. Sites subject to the same zoning as the appraised parcel are usually the most appropriate comparables. If nearby sales in the same zoning category are not available, data from similar multi-unit residential zoning classifications can be used after appropriate adjustments are made. In these situations, the price per square foot of potential apartment unit or price per square foot of potential building area is the key calculation for the subject parcel's value.

For example, a 140-foot by 120-foot site (16,800 square feet) recently sold for $1.2 million. Current zoning allows for a building floor area–to–land area ratio of 6.0:1.0 (usually expressed as 6.0 *FAR*) and a maximum permitted building density of 1 apartment unit per

560 square feet of net rentable area. Two physical land price units that may be calculated for this property are shown below.

$8,571 per front foot ($1,200,000/140 fr. ft.) and

$71.43 per square foot of total land area ($1,200,000/16,800 sq. ft.)

From an economic standpoint, land size per se is relatively unimportant. It is the size of the building, the highest and best use of the site, that dictates the value of the site. The above example is necessarily based on the presumption that prudent use of the site is to fill the available zoning envelope. The indicated building floor area is 100,800 square feet (16,800 square feet x 6.0 *FAR*). If the community interprets net rentable area divided by 80% as equal to building floor area for zoning purposes, in this case, the result is 560/.80 or 700 square feet of floor area per apartment unit. The indicated highest and best use of the 100,800-sq.-ft. building area would be 144 apartments or DUs (dwelling units) (100,800 square feet/700 square feet per apartment unit). This information allows the appraiser to calculate two meaningful building price units:

$8,333 per potential apartment unit ($1,200,000/144 DUs) and

$11.90 per square foot of potential floor area ($1,200,000/100,800 sq. ft.)

This information along with corresponding data for other comparable sales can be displayed and analyzed on a data array grid. Comparative unit prices that conform to a pattern and show the least amount of variance tend to best reflect the thinking of market participants.

Under certain circumstances, an economically feasible or market-preferred density of development is less than the maximum density legally permitted under the zoning. For example, economically unrealistic parking requirements may limit achievable unit density in the apartment building. Nevertheless, in many instances the market bases the value of apartment land on the price per potential apartment unit under the maximum density permitted by the zoning. The market thereby demonstrates that as the unit density or floor area ratio[2] increases, the price per square foot of land area increases while the price per potential apartment unit decreases.

Sources of information on the marketing and transfer of residential income property sites include commercial real estate brokers, apartment developers, lenders, and appraisers who are familiar with sales activity for such parcels. Other sources of data on apartment land sales include records of deeds and assessments, newspapers and real estate business publications, and electronically transmitted sales data services. In addition to recorded sales and signed contracts, an appraiser may also consider asking prices and offers to purchase.

Interviews with sellers, buyers, brokers, lenders, and attorneys involved in the acquisition of a site generally provide the most direct information on the purchase. In confirming the details of a sale with a buyer, it is important to ascertain the motivation behind the

---

2. The floor area ratio (*FAR*) is the relationship between the above-ground floor area of a building and the area of the plot on which it stands; *FAR* is also called *building-to-land ratio*.

purchase as well as the buyer's development plans, particularly with regard to the number and type of apartment units proposed for construction.

Allocation and Extraction

When information on the sales of vacant sites is insufficient, data on improved properties can be used to estimate land value. In both remote rural areas and densely populated urban centers, few, if any, sales of vacant or unimproved sites may be available. Land value can be allocated or extracted on the basis of sales of built-up sites at the time of the sale.

Allocation is especially useful when there is a normal or typical ratio of land value to property value for the given type of apartment property in the subject or comparable neighborhoods. The ratio may be revealed by a pattern in market sales, assessment allocations, and land value–to–property value ratios recognized by local real estate professionals. For example, if research in a multi-unit residential district shows that the site represents 25% of the total property value, an $800,000 sale of an apartment property would indicate a land value of $200,000.

Allocation is most reliable when the land value–to–property value ratio is consistent for similar types of real estate in a defined market area. For example, the subject property is a 15-year-old, 40-unit garden complex located in a neighborhood that is totally developed with rental apartment complexes ranging from 15 to 50 units. The residential rental unit market is currently overbuilt, and no new construction has occurred in the nearby apartment neighborhoods for some time. The local assessor's office has recently reviewed assessments in the subject area, and consequently it is possible to stabilize and update land value–to–property value ratios on the basis of current market conditions. In this case, allocation would probably provide the most accurate indication of land value. However, given the facts in this example, the use of the cost approach would likely be questioned.

When there is no well-defined ratio of land value to total property value among the comparable sale properties, the appraiser may extract site values from comparable sales by estimating the depreciated cost of the improvement and deducting that estimate from the sale price. The difference between the total market price of the property and the depreciated cost estimate of the building is attributable to the land. A value indication based on extraction is generally most conclusive when the building improvements are new and have experienced little depreciation.

An example is provided by the valuation of a vacant site in a fully developed, older apartment neighborhood where there are no unimproved lots and thus no sale/purchase data on sites. In this instance, the appraiser has reason to believe that land value–to–property value ratios in the area are inconsistent. Three improved properties in the immediate vicinity of the site of the subject have recently sold. The sites of these properties are almost identical in size and shape to the site of the subject property, and their highest and best use is also similar to that of the subject. From the sale price of each property, the appraiser deducts the contribution of the depreciated building improvements to establish a range of site value. It can reasonably be assumed that the value of the subject site falls within this range.

In some instances, an indication of overall property value is developed on the basis of income capitalization, but sales comparison and the lack of site sales precludes application of the cost approach. In these cases, it is possible to deduct an estimate of depreciated cost from the property value conclusion to arrive at an estimate of the site value. Such an estimate can be checked against land value–to–property value allocation ratios in otherwise comparable neighborhoods where land sales and property sales both exist.

Land Residual and Ground Rent Capitalization

If it is possible to separate property income into components attributable to the land and the building or if rent for the land is known, direct capitalization procedures can be used to develop an indication of land value.

When income-producing residential properties are sold, it is sometimes possible to isolate the income attributable to the land and capitalize it into an indication of the value of the land as subject to the lease. Conversely, if the income attributable to the improvement(s) is identifiable, it can be capitalized into an indication of the contributory value of the building and deducted from the property's sale price. The residual, or difference between the property's sale price and contributory value of the building, is the value of the land.

Land residual is applicable when the income to either the land or the building can be estimated accurately, a land capitalization rate (R_L) and building capitalization rate (R_B) can be developed from market data, and the overall property income is known or can be estimated.

Ground rent is paid for the right to use and occupy a site according to the terms of a ground lease. Ground rent for the site on which an apartment building is situated can be capitalized by applying an appropriate rate into a value indication of the site as of the effective appraisal date and according to the terms of the lease. The resulting indication reflects the value of the landlord's interest in the land, i.e., the leased fee. If the rent under a ground lease corresponds to market rent as of the effective appraisal date, the value indication developed by application of a market-derived land capitalization rate (R_L) may be equivalent to the fee simple value of the leased land.

As an example, comparable apartment sites in the immediate neighborhood of the subject rent for between $1.40 and $1.50 per square foot of land annually on an absolute net basis (the landlord pays no operating expenses). A highly comparable site of 12,500 square feet recently leased for $18,000 annually, or $1.44 per square foot. Market data suggest an appropriate land capitalization rate for similar properties to be 9.0%. The indicated land value for this site would be $200,000 ($18,000/.09).

Development Cost Estimates

For proposed apartment projects or apartment buildings of recent construction, information on the cost of development is usually both relevant and available for study. Comparable data on expenditures such as construction, carrying, and marketing costs are readily obtainable.

Types of Costs

Some appraisers use the terms *direct costs* or *hard costs* to refer to capital expenditures on labor and materials that are needed to construct the physical improvement. These items include building permits, equipment, fixtures, appliances, utilities installation, contractor's profit, and overhead allowances. In the case of apartment buildings, these expenses can also include the cost of project security during construction and material storage facilities for appliances to be installed in kitchens and bathrooms. *Indirect costs* or *soft costs* include fees for architectural, engineering, consulting, accounting, and legal services; interest on construction loans and financing charges; taxes and required insurance coverage during development; marketing costs (leasing/sales commissions); and administrative expenses. The costs of permanent financing, interest on loans taken to buy land, and processing fees or service charges are other indirect expenses.

In addition to direct and indirect costs, the appraiser recognizes the contribution of the entrepreneur, for which appropriate compensation must be estimated. In an existing project, this expense item is called *entrepreneurial profit;* in a proposed project or one that is near completion but not yet marketed, it is called *entrepreneurial incentive.* Entrepreneurial profit/incentive[3] is a market-derived figure that represents the amount an entrepreneur expects to receive for providing expertise and coordination and for assuming the risk in developing the project. The amount of entrepreneurial profit/incentive varies considerably with market conditions and the basic rent potential of the units in the apartment project.

To estimate this expense item for apartment buildings, an appraiser interviews local developers and real estate professionals to establish a range of anticipated and actual profit characteristics of the market. Entrepreneurial profit/incentive can be estimated as a percentage of direct costs, direct and indirect costs, direct and indirect costs plus land value, or the value of the completed project ("value at stabilization," i.e., sellout or stabilized occupancy), including all costs incurred over the construction and marketing period. Local market practice will dictate the percentage basis to be used. In many apartment markets, entrepreneurial profit/incentive is calculated as a percentage of total direct and indirect costs, which is added to the depreciated value estimate of the improvements. Entrepreneurial profit/incentive is estimated according to rates prevailing in the market as of the effective date of the appraisal.

---

3. When lending institutions and investment firms fulfill the role of an entrepreneur in creating an apartment complex, they usually contract with a developer to manage the project. In these situations, the developer's fee is considered distinct from the entrepreneurial incentive. While an entrepreneur/developer brings time, energy, and expertise to a project and also assumes the risk, he or she may incur considerable administrative overhead as well. Such administrative costs represent development costs and are not considered as part of the entrepreneur's profit.

Reproduction Cost/Replacement Cost

Two bases can be used in developing a value indication by the cost approach. *Reproduction cost* refers to the expenditure required to construct, as of the date of the appraisal, an exact duplicate or replica of the subject structure and the individual units, using the same materials, construction standards, design, and quality of workmanship, and embodying all the deficiencies, superadequacies, and obsolescence of the apartment property being appraised. *Replacement cost,* on the other hand, is the expenditure required to construct an apartment property with utility equivalent to the subject, using current materials and contemporary standards, design, and layout. Because an estimate based on replacement cost tends to eliminate some functional obsolescence, the added costs of removing functionally curable items and possible excess carrying costs incurred by superadequate construction must be considered.

In the valuation of multi-unit residential property, reproduction cost has often been used in the past. The reasons appraisers have followed this practice are threefold:

1. To develop an appropriate analysis of depreciation

2. To suit the preferences of clients, which often are institutions that must comply with appraisal guidelines issued by government agencies

3. To enable the valuer to appraise the actual rather than an equivalent (or replacement) building

Reproduction cost estimates are preferred for multifamily residential properties (often located in older neighborhoods) that evidence functional obsolescence. Even well-built apartment improvements with considerable remaining economic life incur value loss attributable to inutility. These buildings are not likely to be replaced as long as the apartments continue to generate a reasonable income. Because estimates of the functional obsolescence incurred by such buildings are required, the appraiser needs to understand the reproduction basis of cost estimating.

From the point of view of the client, especially a purchaser, an appraisal based on reproduction cost is more useful than replacement cost. In identifying and describing those features of the building and the individual apartment units that the market discounts, such as inadequacies in size or layout and deficiencies in unit placement, the appraiser explains market judgments. Any reductions in value resulting from these unmarketable features are identified as specific depreciation allowances. In a replacement cost estimate they would not be explained.

Because of these advantages, residential appraisal report forms prepared by the Federal National Mortgage Association (FNMA) and the Federal Home Loan Mortgage Corporation (FHLMC) require the use of reproduction cost estimates. Government agencies are aware of the difficulties in estimating replica costs in older structures, and they understand that published or reported figures may often represent hybrids or combinations of reproduction and replacement costs. By specifying a reproduction cost basis, the forms facilitate the complete estimation of depreciation, which accounts for a property's overall loss in value from every known or observable cause. The term *cost new,* or the cost as though the building were new (not when the building was new), was used to ensure that no depreciation was considered in the estimate of costs, and thereby to preclude any *double depreciating*. The term currently favored is simply *cost*. The full amount of value loss is calculated and deducted once all forms of depreciation have been estimated.

Cost Estimating Methods

The most widespread procedure for estimating the construction cost of apartment properties is the comparative unit method. Common units of comparison analyzed in this procedure are cost per apartment unit and cost per square foot of building area. Two other more detailed procedures, the unit-in-place method and quality survey, are also effectively used.

Comparative Unit Method   The comparative unit or comparative square foot method is the most practical and applicable cost technique for valuing apartment properties. Total cost is estimated by comparing the subject apartment building with similar, recently completed buildings for which construction and other development cost data are available. Unit cost figures, which are usually expressed in gross building dimensions, are converted into price per square foot or, in some instances, price per cubic foot. While application of this method usually depends on the availability of data from comparable properties, total cost may also be estimated in the absence of comparable development data. For example, site acquisition prices or site values can be deducted from sale prices of newly constructed apartment projects similar to the subject; the residual figures indicate the development costs, including entrepreneurial profit, for the comparable buildings. Alternative sources of data on comparative unit costs include manuals that publish cost data on benchmark or prototype buildings and professional cost analysts with expertise in developing estimates based on building plans or specifications.

When similar apartment buildings are in the planning or construction stage, it may be possible to obtain comparative construction cost data through interviews with contractors, developers, accountants, lenders, architects, assessors, and other officials in local government. This information can be quoted simply as the fees paid the general contractor, subcontractors, and tradesmen, as the cost per square foot of gross building area, or as cost per apartment unit. Occasionally, it is possible to obtain building cost data itemized on the basis of materials and labor. Local developers and local builders are especially good sources on current apartment building costs. The builder's or architect's job cost sheet can provide benchmark data on expenditures for structures of similar design, building materials, quality of construction, and number of rental units. Current job cost files, however, are the property of the contractor and are not always available to an appraiser. Job cost files for recently completed and marketed buildings are likely to be more readily available.

Appraisers specializing in apartment valuation maintain ongoing records for use as comparative cost data and for evaluating the applicability of information from published cost services to local market figures. Calculations of the local construction cost per building component or per rental unit can be compared against national averages. The cost of a building as estimated by an appraiser is a typical or average calculation that is not representative of the specific costs of any one builder or apartment project. Factors such as the contractor's scale of operation, the date the site and materials were acquired, or differences among the construction and installation methods employed produce variations in cost among typical or similar buildings. The published cost services provide guidelines for adjusting typical national averages to regional development norms.

In the absence of data from direct comparison or job cost files, it may be possible to extract an indication of the total cost of an apartment building from sales of newly completed structures. The residual remaining after deducting site value from the sale price of a newly constructed comparable provides an indication of the total cost of the building. This method of cost comparison is valid when the comparable improvement represents the highest and best use of the site, the property has achieved stabilized occupancy, the transacted price reflects a balanced supply-demand equation, and the market value of the site is reasonably ascertainable. The indicated cost, including all component expenditures as well as entrepreneurial profit, is then calculated as a single cost per unit—e.g., cost per square foot of gross building area, finished gross building area, net building area, or cost per apartment unit. A single-dollar average of construction cost per square foot may not fully account for differences in quality, design, and apartment number and size. And unit prices sometimes need to be appropriately revised if market support for adjustments is available. The best unit price estimates, therefore, are based on cost comparables that are very similar to the subject.

Alternative Sources of Data for Comparative Unit Analysis   Another way of developing a comparative unit cost estimate is to use data from recognized cost services. These publications report current costs per square foot as national averages for standard building designs according to different categories of construction quality. Some services provide many, if not all, development costs; others limit their data to construction costs. Cost manuals contain segregated or segmented cost information, i.e., unit costs of specific components as installed in various categories of benchmark or prototype buildings. Usually, the unit costs are provided for a base structure of specified size, to which the appraiser makes additions or deductions to approximate the actual area or volume of the subject improvement. Proper use of cost service data requires that the appraiser understand which items are included in the base cost and which are excluded. In accordance with economies of scale, the unit cost tends to be lower when a subject building is larger than the benchmark building; conversely, the unit cost is likely to be higher when the subject is smaller.

Cost services that publish printed data (or make the data available on-line) generally provide updates over the course of the year, and some data are revised monthly or quarterly. However, published data should be checked frequently against costs in the local market. Cost services also report periodic changes in the cost index occurring since a given base year. The appraiser can apply this figure to the historical cost of the subject building, as reported by accounting firms in a note to the owner's balance sheet, for the period that has passed since the subject was completed.

Among appraisers of apartment buildings, there are two schools of thought. Some favor data from local cost comparables; others prefer published cost service data. The proponents of using local cost comparables believe that variances are so great nationally that the average figures compiled by cost services rarely relate to the local market. Those who advocate using cost manuals contend that market thinking is better represented by published figures on average costs and that multipliers or adjustments can be effectively applied to offset differences between the components in the subject and those of a benchmark building. Most appraisers agree, however, that primary cost data should be site-specific and that published cost manuals are better used to substantiate and confirm primary data.

Automated computer programs are available for the mechanical calculations required in a segregated cost analysis, which is developed on the basis of the user's response to questions posed by the software. Automated services also furnish current cost information and can prepare detailed estimates at greater speed and less expense than is possible by hand.

Breakdown Cost Calculations A cost analyst using the unit-in-place or segregated cost method calculates the separate cost of each major physical component in a building, e.g., the foundations, walls, floors, ceilings, roof, and heating systems. The estimate for each item includes the cost of constructing, attaching, or installing the component, but not non-construction items such as indirect costs. In a multibuilding apartment project, the unit-in-place method can be applied to either the entire complex or the individual structures. Cost analysts who perform this type of analysis have specialized knowledge of construction. Using this method, it is possible to estimate construction costs in greater detail than can be done for total cost by the broader comparative unit method. The unit-in-place method is also useful for identifying the quality of structural components and calculating needed capital expenditures. It is often employed to modify or adjust estimates developed by the comparative unit method and to estimate costs of rehabilitation. As a primary cost-estimating method, unit-in-place is especially applicable to older apartment buildings for which it would be difficult to make accurate estimates on the basis of cost comparables.

A quantity survey is the most comprehensive method for estimating cost. It is a detailed, complex, and time-consuming activity that requires special expertise. It too is restricted to developing estimates of construction costs. The quantity and quality of all materials used and all categories of labor required are reflected in the quantity survey. Unit costs are applied to quantities of materials and labor hours to estimate the total cost of materials and labor. To this amount are added margins for the contractor, contingency fees, overhead, and profit. A cost expert must have access to written specifications and construction drawings before the quantity survey can be prepared. A trained cost estimator is usually retained if the character of the improvements or the nature of the appraisal assignment requires a complete building cost breakdown. A quantity survey is usually the basis for contractors' bids, but the method is seldom used by appraisers except in the case of highly customized properties or properties with unique features and where the cost approach is the most heavily weighted valuation approach.

Site Improvement Costs   In addition to the main building or buildings, cost estimates made for appraisals of apartment properties must include the costs of improvements to the site such as parking structures or compounds, walks and driveways, fences and walls, pools, patios, outside lighting, and landscaping. The cost of landscaping and other site improvements often varies considerably. For practical reasons, therefore, many appraisers estimate the contributory value of these items rather than their depreciated cost. For example, the value of a swimming pool can be estimated by calculating the amount of additional rent paid by tenants because the pool is included among the common facilities available.

Estimating Depreciation

Depreciation is the difference between the cost to create or recreate an improvement and its market value, both estimated as of the effective date of the appraisal. The depreciation estimate reflects market perceptions and is a penalty on value only insofar as it is recognized by the market. In fact, some physical imperfections, design flaws, or locational blight may be overlooked by buyers.[4] The appraiser's basic tasks are to consider the property's condition or specific features thereof that may cause a loss in value, and then to measure the diminution in value attributable to these causes.

Physical Deterioration

Among the various factors that account for the depreciation of apartment buildings over time is physical deterioration. As a building ages, it is subject to wear and tear resulting from human use as well as the impact of the elements. Effective maintenance or building administration may slow down the deterioration process while neglect or poor upkeep usually accelerates it. In apartment buildings, physical deterioration can be kept in check by weather stripping (thin metal or wood stripping installed between the joints of doors and window casings to keep out the elements), storm windows, insulation, and proper placement of the building on the site. When the correction of physical deterioration is deferred, the process by which the property loses value is accelerated.

---

4. The subject of depreciation is controversial. Some theorists argue that even a newly constructed building of perfect design and ideal location suffers some incurable functional obsolescence because eventually it will have to be torn down. Yet, since the date of ultimate demolition is indeterminable, it is virtually impossible to estimate a charge for depreciation by discounting the cost to present value. Similarly, other theorists claim that in a reproduction cost estimate, excavation should not be included among the building costs for which depreciation is estimated since an excavated site is not subject to wear. Market thinking in both cases tends to dismiss such arguments. The market only considers the present value of the cost of eventual demolition near the end of a building's economic life. The market also recognizes that excavation costs contribute proportionately less as time goes on.

The appraiser develops an understanding of the maintenance level and condition of the building by carefully inspecting a representative sample of the individual units as well as the public areas and mechanical systems. A significant degree of exterior damage is often the result of inadequate security provided by the property manager. Other examples of physical deterioration are insect or pest infestation and the presence of contaminated materials or environmental hazards. Since these factors have a different effect on each part of the apartment building, the loss in value is analyzed via specific components, although this loss may be reported on a general basis.

Functional Obsolescence

A building suffers functional obsolescence due to some flaw in the structure, building materials, or design that diminishes its functionality, utility, and hence its value. Functional obsolescence is caused by dated features of older buildings even if the apartment units are still in good repair and sound physical condition. However, a newly constructed rental complex can also include functional obsolescence in the form of a deficient floor plan or an awkward traffic flow.

Included among the value losses experienced by many apartment projects that can be attributed to functional inutility are an inappropriate unit mix, restrictive apartment sizes, and defective unit placement. Kitchen appliances and bathroom fixtures of unacceptable quality or outmoded design frequently lower the potential rent the apartments can command. Multistory buildings may suffer from outdated or nonexistent elevators; lack of on-site parking; too few windows; limited balcony or patio space; inadequate heating, plumbing, and electrical systems; and insufficient laundry, storage, or service areas.

External Obsolescence

A building suffers from external obsolescence when negative influences off-site impair the utility or marketability of the property. Generally, these influences are incurable on the part of the landlord, owner, or tenant. Adverse market conditions are a common cause of this kind of obsolescence. For example, high mortgage interest rates may preclude redevelopment or cause the current costs of renovation to exceed the amount warranted by additional income from building rents. Local overbuilding that creates a surplus of available apartments will negatively affect rent potential. Locational problems include hazardous traffic conditions, nonconforming zoning, inharmonious land uses in the vicinity, physical obstacles impeding access, and local nuisances such as unpleasant odors or noise. For external obsolescence to cause a loss in building value, however, the amount of value loss to the overall property must exceed the component of the loss that can be attributed to the site as though it were vacant.

Methods of Estimating Depreciation

The four methods of estimating depreciation are economic age-life, modified economic age-life, sales comparison, and the breakdown method. After developing the estimate of depreciation, the appraiser deducts it from the cost of the existing improvements to arrive at their contribution to property value. In the appraisal of apartment properties, the more common procedures of estimating depreciation are economic age-life and sales comparison.

Age-Life Concepts

Several age-life concepts must be grasped before the relevant age-life procedure can be carried out. These include economic life, useful life, remaining economic life, and remaining useful life.

Economic life is the period of time when the improvements contribute to the market value of the property, which is necessarily more than the value contribution of the site. The economic life of a building begins when it is completed and ends when the property value no longer exceeds the value of the site. In terms of income, the total net rent generated by the apartments must exceed the return that could be expected from the site alone. When an apartment building has reached the end of its economic life, the underlying land parcel (as though vacant) would likely sell for more than the property with the existing improvement, the cost of demolition being considered.

The useful life of a building is the period of time over which the physical components of the improvement are reasonably expected to perform the functions for which they were designed. Physical components made of steel and concrete have useful lives that could last for hundreds of years, but it is unlikely that the improvements of which they form a part will have such long economic expectancies. Useful life and economic life can differ widely, and useful life typically exceeds economic life. A building can be used beyond the date it contributes to value.

The longevity of apartment buildings is considered in terms of both actual age (that is, historical or chronological age) and effective age (age indicated by the condition and quality of the structure). The actual age of a building is the number of years that have elapsed since construction was completed; it is an established fact, whereas the effective age is an estimate based on physical condition as observed by the appraiser. Because apartment buildings of the same actual age may vary in condition and desirability due to differences in maintenance, management, and upgrades, appraisers base depreciation estimates on the effective age rather than the actual age of the structure. Rehabilitating or remodeling an older building usually lengthens the economic life and nearly always extends the useful life[5] while reducing its effective age.

The remaining economic life of a building is its total anticipated economic life less its effective age. In other words, remaining economic life is an estimate, as of the effective date of the appraisal, of the period over which the rental units will continue to contribute to

---

5. The economic age-life method uses the ratio of effective age to anticipated total economic life to derive a lump-sum estimate of depreciation in the building. The useful age-life ratio, or ratio of actual age to anticipated total useful life, lends itself only to the age-life procedure for estimating physical deterioration. Estimates of total useful life may be difficult to support.

overall property value. This period begins on the effective date of the valuation and extends until the end of the building's economic life. Remaining economic life is always less than, or equal to, but never more than total economic life. The existing condition of the property reflected by the rental value of the apartments is considered in estimating both effective age and remaining economic life. The remaining useful life is the estimated period from the actual age of a physical component of the building to the end of its total useful life expectancy. The remaining useful life of any long-lived component is equal to or, typically, greater than the remaining economic life.

In estimating the economic life of a building, the appraiser investigates the ages at which similar buildings are demolished and the economic life expectancies of structures that are comparable to the subject and located in its market area. The quality of construction and functional utility are taken into account. Although the economic expectancy of an apartment building is difficult to predict, several considerations guide the appraiser in arriving at an estimate. Physical considerations include the rate at which building components wear out, given the construction quality, the type of tenants residing in the apartments, and the standards of maintenance and management. Functional considerations pertain to the rapidity of change in construction techniques, tenant tastes, and typical household size and composition. External considerations are generally economic, relating to long-term influences such as the stage in the neighborhood's life cycle and the ability of the apartment buildings in the neighborhood to attract tenants at appropriate rents. The economic life of a building can cease because its site and similar sites have become more valuable for another land use.

Because many of these factors become more significant only over the course of future years, economic life expectancy is difficult to forecast accurately. Nevertheless, market study and analysis of trends may provide the needed information on which to base an economic life estimate. This is true for calculations of remaining economic life as well. The maintenance standards of managers and tenants can influence the rate of a building's physical deterioration. If the apartments are better maintained than others in the market area, the effective age of the building will be less than its actual age. If a 30-year-old apartment complex has been exceptionally managed and maintained, the apartment units will command market rents typical of competing units that are 10 years younger, and the effective age of the subject property would be estimated as 20 years. Comparison of rental rates is usually a reliable method of analyzing the effective age of apartment projects.

Economic Age-Life Method

The economic age-life method identifies the rate at which comparable apartments depreciate. This rate, along with the effective age of the subject units, is used to estimate depreciation. Through research of comparables, the appraiser identifies the anticipated total economic life of similar apartment complexes in the market area and also estimates the effective age of the subject building units. The ratio that results from dividing the effective age of the subject by the anticipated total economic life of comparable buildings is applied to the cost of the subject to provide a lump-sum estimate of depreciation. The depreciation estimate is then deducted from the total cost of the building improvement(s). The lump-sum estimate obtained incorporates all forms of depreciation that may be present—physical deterioration and functional and economic obsolescence—but the overall estimate is not disaggregated according to type of depreciation.

For example, a 20-year-old building containing 35 units recently underwent a major rehabilitation program. The kitchens and bathrooms in each apartment were modernized. The building is now fully leased at rental rates that correspond to those generated by competitive apartments constructed about 12 years ago in the immediate market area. These structures have been maintained in average to good condition. Their anticipated total economic life is projected to be approximately 60 years, which is typical of economic-life expectancy in the neighborhood. In this case, the indicated rate of depreciation is estimated at 12/60 or 20%.

Modified Economic Age-Life Method

The economic age-life method may be modified to segment out from the subject's cost all items of depreciation that are curable. The appraiser begins by estimating the cost to cure items of physical deterioration resulting from deferred maintenance and items of curable functional obsolescence. Total curable depreciation is deducted from the cost of the subject improvement(s) as of the effective date of the appraisal. The appraiser then applies an adjusted economic age-life ratio to the remaining cost (or depreciated cost) to arrive at a lump-sum estimate of depreciation. The modified economic age-life method recognizes that when curable items are corrected, remaining economic life usually increases and effective age is reduced. It closely approximates the reasoning of informed buyers who wish to know how much the units will be worth after all curable problems have been attended to. Most astute buyers will be concerned with the potential income after repairs have been made rather than the income generated by the property in its present depreciated state.

Sales Comparison Method

Sales comparison is usually a reliable procedure for estimating depreciation in apartment buildings, provided sufficient sales data are available to support the appraiser's conclusion. This method explicitly recognizes that loss in value reflects the perceptions of buyers and sellers in the market. It is based on the premise that if old apartment buildings are worth less than new buildings, they will sell for less.

The appraiser begins by deducting the land value from the sale price of each comparable to arrive at the depreciated value of the improvement. The cost of each comparable building is estimated, and the depreciated value of the improvement is deducted from the cost estimate. The remainder is a lump-sum dollar estimate of depreciation.

The dollar amount can be converted into a percentage by dividing each estimate of depreciation by the cost of the building. An average annual depreciation rate may be obtained by dividing each total depreciation percentage by the actual age of the building.

Since depreciation does not necessarily accrue on a straight-line basis (indeed, many buildings tend to depreciate more rapidly as they approach the end of their economic lives), it should not be inferred that the building depreciated at the annual average rate.

If, for example, a 10-year-old comparable had sold for $4.8 million and the value of the land was estimated as $1.6 million, the depreciated value of the building would be $3.2 million. Assuming that the cost of the comparable as of the effective date of the appraisal was $4 million, the total depreciation indicated would be $800,000, the difference between the cost ($4 million) and the depreciated value ($3.2 million). Dividing $800,000 by the cost ($800,000/$4,000,000) results in a depreciation rate of 20%, and an average annual depreciation rate is calculated as 2% (20%/10 years).

The more dissimilar the comparable properties are from the subject in terms of costs and the types/amount of depreciation, the less reliable are the depreciation indications obtained from sales comparison. Another potential difficulty in applying this method is a paucity of market evidence for land values. In older residential districts, information is often available on sale prices and construction costs of comparable apartment buildings, but land sales are rare. Despite such limitations, many appraisers believe that sales comparison provides extremely reliable and persuasive results and prefer this method for estimating depreciation in apartment buildings.

Breakdown Method

The breakdown method is the most detailed and comprehensive procedure for estimating and reporting depreciation. The appraiser analyzes each potential cause of depreciation separately and estimates its impact on value. Once all the estimates have been made, they are added up and the total lump-sum depreciation figure is deducted from the cost of the improvement(s). Appropriate methods are used to estimate the depreciation attributable to each of the following categories and subcategories.

Physical deterioration is considered either curable or incurable at the time of the appraisal. Curable deterioration includes items that need immediate attention, e.g., items of deferred maintenance, cosmetic upgrades (touch-up painting), or electrical and plumbing repairs. Curable deterioration is estimated by the current cost to cure the specific item in the most feasible manner. By contrast, items of incurable deterioration do not need immediate attention, only normal maintenance. These items can be repaired in the future or else are short-lived items that can be replaced at some later time. Examples of incurable deterioration include roof and floor coverings, exterior painting, plumbing fixtures, kitchen appliances, and heating units. Incurable deterioration is estimated as the partial wear incurred by the specific component. The appraiser applies a useful age-life ratio, the ratio of actual age to anticipated total useful life, to the cost of the deteriorated item, which may be short-lived or long-lived. To estimate incurable deterioration for all long-lived or structural components of the building, the useful age-life ratio is applied to the cost of the building, less the physical depreciation estimated for curable and incurable short-lived items.

Functional obsolescence is also considered either curable or incurable. The test of economic feasibility determines whether the functional obsolescence is curable or incurable. Functional obsolescence is further differentiated according to cause, that is, a deficiency or a superadequacy.

Curable functional obsolescence arises from deficiencies requiring additions (the need to install a wheelchair ramp or automatic elevator controls) or substitution/modernization (the need to replace asbestos pipe insulation). Curable obsolescence requiring an addition is calculated as the excess cost of adding the item over the cost of including the item with new construction. Curable deficiencies requiring substitution of components (e.g., new fixtures) already included in the cost estimate are measured as the cost of installing the new component minus the salvage value of the existing component.

Estimates of curable functional obsolescence resulting from a superadequacy vary depending on whether the basis of the cost estimate is reproduction or replacement cost. This is because certain superadequacies are eliminated in replacement cost estimates and no charge for obsolescence is therefore deducted. In reproduction cost estimates, curable functional obsolescence due to a superadequacy is the reproduction cost of the item as included in the cost estimate, minus the physical deterioration already deducted, minus the cost to cure, i.e., the cost to replace[6] a superadequate item with a standard item or to refinish superadequate space. An example is a water fountain located on the center island of a circular driveway at the entrance to the apartment complex. Because of depleted water reserves, the community bans its use. The fountain is removed and the plot is landscaped.

Incurable functional obsolescence is also differentiated according to its cause, which may be a deficiency or a superadequacy. If a deficiency in the existing structure, such as poor floor plan in the apartment units, is not economically feasible to cure, it is estimated as the net income loss attributable to the deficiency, capitalized at the building capitalization rate. The same procedure applies to any deficiency arising from the absence of a component that should have been included in the building, but the cost of which is not included in the reproduction cost.

Incurable functional obsolescence resulting from a superadequacy that would not now be included in the building, but the cost of which is included in the reproduction cost, is estimated as the cost, less the physical deterioration already charged, less the discounted value of any added costs of ownership (maintenance, insurance, property taxes), less the value added by the item (increased rent), if appropriate. Alternatively, incurable functional obsolescence can be estimated as the value of the loss attributable to the superadequacy, capitalized at the building capitalization rate. Examples include an incinerator whose operation is no longer permitted and hardwood floors in the lobby that are covered with wall-to-wall carpeting. The test of curability indicates these items are incurable because no economic gain would offset the cost of removing them.

External obsolescence is a loss in value caused by factors outside the property. It is

---

6. This includes the costs of removal and installation, minus any salvage value in the old component.

generally considered as incurable on the part of the owner, landlord, or tenants since they cannot cure it. For apartment properties, external obsolescence is estimated by capitalizing the loss in the property's net income due to the off-site condition and then deducting the component of this loss that is attributable to the land. (The land value estimate already reflects the diminution in value due to this cause.) Causes of external obsolescence could include nearby adverse land uses or a perception of high street crime. The result is neighborhood decline, which prevents the apartment units from commanding competitive rental rates.

Application

Table 6.1 provides a summation of depreciation analyzed by breakdown procedures. The 62-unit subject property contains 35,400 finished square feet. With an actual age of 15 years, the property has received a level of maintenance that is standard for its market. The effective age is estimated to be the same as the actual age (15 years). The property's economic life expectancy is 50 years.

Table 6.1 Cost Approach Summary

Reproduction Cost of the Improvements

Direct Costs (General Contract)			$1,861,000
Indirect Costs			
Architectural and Engineering	$200,000		
Financing	330,000		
Marketing	30,000		
Legal, Accounting, Appraisal	60,000		
Miscellaneous	+ 5,000		
		$625,000	
Entrepreneurial Profit		+ 282,000	
			$2,768,000

Depreciation

Physical Deterioration			
Curable		$85,000	
Incurable			
Short-lived	$224,000		
Long-lived	+ 156,000		
		+ $380,000	
			$465,000

Table 6.1 Cost Approach Summary (continued)

Functional Obsolescence

Curable

Deficiency	$20,000		
Superadequacy	+ 50,000		
		$70,000	

Incurable

Deficiency	$55,000		
Superadequacy	+ 75,000		
		+ $130,000	
		$200,000	
External Obsolescence		+ 158,000	
Total Depreciation			− $823,000
Value of the Depreciated Improvements			$1,945,000
Value of the Land			+ 600,000
Value of the Fee Simple Real Estate			$2,545,000
Value of the Personal Property Included			+ 25,000
Total Value Indicated by the Cost Approach			$2,570,000

Notes: Total curable depreciation comes to $155,000, total incurable depreciation to $668,000.

Total depreciation is about 30% of reproduction cost.

Land value is 18% of the sum of the cost of the property (reproduction cost plus land value: $2,768,000 + $600,000 = $3,368,000); land value is about 24% of the value of the fee simple real estate.

The value of the personal property included is about 1% of total property value.

CHAPTER 7

Reconciling, Reporting, and Reviewing

This chapter covers three distinct but inter-related topics: 1) a field appraiser reconciles the appraisal analysis and 2) reports the appraisal opinion; 3) another professional, a review appraiser, then analyzes the field appraiser's report.

Reconciling

The late James Graaskamp, longtime professor at the University of Wisconsin, defined the art of appraisal as the process of screening alternatives. Especially in the reconciliation step, through the screening process, the appraiser resolves differences among the alternative valuation indications so that each reinforces the appraiser's final value opinion.

To analyze is to divide a complex whole into its components in order to determine its essential composition or nature. The final step in the development of a market value opinion is to analyze the preliminary conclusions of the independently developed valuation approaches selected for the particular assignment. In so doing, the appraiser will confront ostensibly conflicting results, reconcile those differences, and reach a defensible final appraisal opinion.

The appraiser's final opinion of value may be, but is not necessarily, equal to the conclusion of one of the valuation approaches. However, it would be highly unusual for this final opinion of value to lie outside the range of value indicated by the results of the valuation approaches applied.

Residential rental property comes in all shapes and sizes. Field appraisers do not always follow consistent methodologies, so the review appraiser's job is an essential quality control function.

The final opinion itself can be a range between two specified dollar amounts. In such a case, the extremes of the range may lie outside the range formed by the point conclusions of the individual valuation approaches. Real estate transactions (e.g., purchases, mortgages, takings), as well as surrogate transactions (e.g., assessments, casualty losses, letters of credit) customarily require a precise dollar amount. Even in cases in which the quantity of apartment land is unknown, requiring a price adjustment to be established by a post-contract survey, a precise per-acre amount will be established. For the client's convenience, most value appraisals are expressed as a precise amount (point estimate) rather than a value range. Whereas the result of an appraiser's valuation process is understood to be the appraiser's best estimate (but one that is possibly in error), the implication of, and justifica-tion for, a value range is its superior degree of accuracy. The wider the range, of course, the greater its accuracy, but it is equally true that a wide range is less useful to the client.

Probability ranges, as distinct from value ranges, are attempts to quantify the degree of error that is statistically likely when extending a sample of data; the quantity of data available for a typical apartment house appraisal will be insufficient for such statistical analysis. Appraisers occasionally are asked to include an ancillary exercise with an apartment property's valuation that is akin to probability analysis. For example, the appraiser may be asked to calculate the amount that the value would be if the hypothetical market rent were to exceed the actual market rent to a specified extent. Under such conditions, the appraiser might be invited to include a subjectively derived probability rating to estimate the odds that the inflated amount used in the calculation will actually be attained. It is unclear how such calculations might be used, and apprais-ers should undertake such assignments only after consulting the Uniform Standards of Professional Appraisal Practice regarding the need to avoid issuing unsupported esti-mates and misleading opinions.

The Valuation Process

Reconciliation, in addition to being a step in the development of a valuation opinion, is a section of most written (and many oral) valuation appraisal reports of apartment properties. In preparation for the reconciliation section of the report, it is only natural to make notes, list key phrases, and outline the thought process followed in developing the final value conclusion. Often, appraisers have drafted much of the appraisal report before they have completed the reconciliation thought process. It is quite natural, then, that portions of the appraisal report (draft and final) be examined as part of the reconciliation.

For a typical apartment property, the appraiser may reconcile as many as nine preliminary value indications or as few as two. In an extreme case, the results of three income capitaliza-tion approach procedures (cash flow discounting, net income capitalization, and gross income multiplier), four sales approach procedures (per apartment, per room, per gross square foot, and per net square foot), and two cost approach indications (land as a vacant site and summation including the depreciated improvements) could be considered. Another method is to reconcile the various income conclusions and the four sales conclusions within their respective approaches, restricting the final reconciliation to a single indication from each approach. When the approaches employed provide adequate evidence that the improvements make a significant value contribution, no further consideration need be given to the value of the land. However, if the indicated total value as improved is less than, equal to, or only slightly more than the land value, that fact will result in possible conflicts to be reconciled. For example, site-size adjustments to rental comparables and to sale comparables should be reexamined, and the periodic rehabilitation costs projected in the DCF should be reconsidered.

The Market

The relationship between the market data used within the various approaches and the correlation among the approaches is another focus in reconciliation. For example, assume the appraiser has determined that market trends are favorable and has forecast that they will continue. The conclusions derived from the approaches could be inconsistent if the results of the trend-inflated comparable sales are accepted in the sales comparison approach while adjustments are made to the capitalization rates extracted from these sales in the income capitalization approach.

Criteria

As part of reconciliation, the appraiser will consider the relative strengths and weaknesses of the approaches being reconciled. Considerations here include how the market perceives the merit of each approach, the quantity of accurate and detailed data supporting each approach, and the appraiser's judgment of the appropriateness of each approach. Throughout the reconciliation process, there is a natural temptation to favor the results of the approach with the most detailed data or the most successful scientific manipulation of data. On the other hand, when reconciling appraisal approaches for a typical apartment property valuation, the appraiser's professional task is not to process data, adjust comparables, or fulfill a checklist. It is to arrive at an accurate value estimate that

1. Is logical

2. Seems reasonable and consistent with all the information provided

3. Is arithmetically sound

4. Is the result of properly selected and executed techniques

5. Seems representative of the inspected property, its location and marketplace, and the use to which the appraisal is to be put

Whereas contradictory information is not meant to thwart the appraiser's arrival at an accurate valuation, it cannot be ignored. Even contradicting data should be confronted in the reconciliation process.

Points of View

As an example of reconciliation, assume an appraiser has used three procedures in the appraisal of an apartment property with the following results:

Method 1: $887,000

Method 2: $908,000

Method 3: $900,000

In reconciling the three preliminary conclusions, the appraiser has observed that the strongest approach is the one producing the $887,000 indication, whereas the weakest approach indicates $900,000. After considering all the information, the appraiser has concluded that the final estimate of value is $900,000—coincidental with, but not because of, the weakest approach.

Other appraisers might have used round numbers, such as the following:

Method 1: $890,000

Method 2: $910,000

Method 3: $900,000

The rounding of these results may seem a little contrived and may inadvertently introduce an arithmetic bias in that it increases two of the indications. Otherwise, however, rounding has no impact on the appraiser's opinion of $900,000.

Another appraiser might round each of the two extreme indications by about 1%, to $900,000, which would require explaining the rounding and obviate explaining the differences in the approaches. Such a procedure would tend to mask the fact that the conclusion of the weakest approach and the final conclusion are equal.

An appraiser could legitimately reach a final conclusion of $887,000, the result of the strongest approach. It is a philosophical difference that separates one appraiser's selection of $900,000 and another's selection of $887,000. Psychological reasoning could also play a role in the reconciliation inasmuch as the two numbers are less than 1.5% apart. For example, when appraising in an adversarial matter for a client whose interest would be furthered by a high value conclusion, an appraiser might choose the lower $887,000 conclusion (from the strongest approach) in order to enhance the credibility of the appraisal.

No completed approach is likely to be so weak that it must be discarded completely in reconciliation. On the other hand, an appraisal approach may have been omitted altogether as inappropriate. For example, assume the highest and best use of an apartment property's site (as though it were a vacant lot) is speculative holding rather than immediate construction. In this case, applying the cost approach to value the property as improved with the existing apartment building would be inappropriate. A well-informed person acting for self-interest would not now develop the site. No construction is the highest and best use. In other words, the highest and best use and the cost approach are in conflict. Similarly, when the highest and best use of a site is to leave it unimproved for the foreseeable future, a land residual technique is not a valid method for estimating market value. This technique may be employed to estimate the use value of a parcel of land, however, when the highest and best use is speculative holding rather than immediate development. For example, the land residual technique is used in the appraisal of the reuse value of apartment land as defined by HUD for urban renewal purposes.

Value Allocation

The appraiser's final value estimate of an apartment property may include personalty as well as realty. If so, the personalty must be identified and its effect on the value considered; an obvious way of accomplishing both is by allocation. For example, the income to be capitalized into value may arise from occupancy of both furnished and unfurnished apartments. Tenants are attracted to the premises by, among other amenities, the professional landscaping, the concierge staff in the lobby that provides numerous personal services and bills by the month, and the optional maid service available through management on either a regular or an occasional basis. In such a case, it is likely that the value of the appraised property exceeds the contribution to value made by the land and building components. It is possible to allocate the income from a going concern among its various components and select and apply separate appropriate capitalization rates to produce the value of each component. This procedure is similar to that often used when appraising leased fee and leasehold interests. Regarding personal property/real property allocations, however, it is more common to first capitalize all the income and then allocate the capitalized value.

The reasons for allocating the appraised value between real and personal property are pragmatic. The client's intended use of the appraisal often requires that the value contribution of the various components be identified. A mortgage lender may wish to confine loan collateral to real estate; a casualty insurance carrier may wish to confine coverage to tangible property; an eminent domain condemnor may be required to exclude furniture and working capital items from the estimated just compensation; an accountant may need to establish explicit depreciation schedules to reduce income tax liability; or an assessor will want to assign the correct proportion of price to taxable assets.

To the extent that contributing personal property is not segregated from the total, it obviously inflates the residual and could be mistakenly allocated to land and improvements. Also, when the allocation between real and personal property is not done, users have a more difficult time understanding the appraiser's opinion of whether a personalty item is inadequate, appropriate, or superadequate from the standpoints of rental competition, appearance, operating efficiency, modernity, fashion, or fad.

Some apartment appraisals include personalty, others do not. In either case, the client is likely to find it helpful if the real property value is allocated between land and improvements. In most such cases, the land value allocation would be its market value as though it were a vacant lot available for development with its highest and best use. The allocation process, too, should reconcile differences in appraisal procedure (if any) regarding surplus land when appropriate.

Working Capital   One class of real estate-related personalty can be working capital, i.e., such liquid asset items as tools, supplies, uniforms, fuel, net receivables, and, of course, cash and bank accounts. Sometimes a corporation or a limited partnership will be the subject of sale rather than the apartment property that is its only asset. In the sale of the real estate, but not in the sale of its owning business entity, working capital items are often treated as cash adjustments on the settlement sheet, in which case the appraisal should exclude these items. Ordinarily, each item of working capital is allocated either as it appears on the grantor's balance sheet or as an amount equal to its off-site salvage value, depending upon whether the highest and best use is to retain or dispose of the item. For example, if the motivation for acquisition, and the best use, is to expand the purchaser's holdings, some of the acquired facility's equipment might be surplus. If the highest and best use is to keep the traditional name of the property, it may be prudent to retain the employees' uniforms, at least temporarily.

Goodwill   Another personal property item that may have a zero value, but alternatively may make a significant contribution to value, is goodwill, which is variously explained as the synergy arising from able direction of an enterprise or the result of such synergy which is a larger-than-average profit margin. Goodwill is intangible; its existence is represented by such evidence as

- Contracts with suppliers of goods, services, and labor
- Hiring, training, and retaining competent employees
- Former public relations efforts, possibly enhanced by advertising
- An occupancy waiting list

Goodwill is a function of success; its allocation can be calculated as a factor applied to gross or net income. If it exists, goodwill is part of capital value imputable to the physical, possessory, and financial interests. It should not be confused with management fees, which are expenses paid to employees, contractors, or agents of the parties. The value of an appraisal practice, for example, may be enhanced by the energy, efficiency, integrity, and intellect of the office manager. The office manager's salary quantifies the basis for the enhanced value of the business, but it is not the measure of the enhancement.

Goodwill is sometimes referred to as *going value, going concern,* and *going business.* However, those terms are also used to mean the entire operation, including, but not merely, its intangible component. Goodwill is generally the most risk-laden of the value components because events, including those beyond the control of management, can cause goodwill to abruptly atrophy or cease. A spate of assaults at an apartment project, for example, if widely reported, could erode the property's reputation as both a place to live and a place to work. A tragedy resulting from management lapses regarding a locked fire exit or a careless swimming pool lifeguard, or notoriety arising from a sanitation infraction or an accusation of illegal prejudice can diminish the investment reputation of an apartment property.

Furniture, Fixtures, and Equipment Of the categories of personal property, FF&E often makes the greatest value contribution. Some divide FF&E into three categories:

1. Furniture, or easily movable contents with economic lives exceeding one year (i.e., not including supplies and inventories that are part of working capital).

2. Trade fixtures, or items connected, constructed, or installed with ultimate removal in mind. (Items installed by apartment tenants with the implicit understanding that they will retain ownership are called *domestic fixtures* and are not included in the fixtures category.)

3. Equipment, vehicles, and machines such as devices for bookkeeping, communicating, laundering, waxing, vacuuming, etc.

In practice, however, FF&E items are often grouped because distinguishing them into three categories promotes controversy with no offsetting advantage.

The allocation of furniture, fixtures, and equipment generally covers items that taken together contribute to the operation of the premises. To the extent that the highest and best use requires the replacement of an item, its value contribution is confined to the amount that would be paid in the open market for the item as is, where is, and for off-site removal at the cost to the purchaser. Many real estate appraisers retain FF&E valuers to advise them regarding replacement cost, physical condition, operating efficiency, and available salvage price and scrap price—information which is helpful to the appraiser when determining contributory market value.

Other sources of information regarding FF&E include the accountant's balance sheet notes, the owner's acquisition records, interviews with management, and, of course, the condition observed during the appraiser's inspection.

Reporting

The verb *appraise* means to estimate value; there is no expressed or implied restriction that limits the type of value or the definition of the specified value. The noun *appraisal* means the appraiser's opinion of value, i.e., the value amount the appraiser has estimated. A professional appraiser's estimates of value are to be impartially and competently formed and clearly reported so as to not mislead anyone who might be influenced by the report.

The licensing authorities of some states have preserved the traditional distinction between *appraisal* and *appraisal report* that is embodied within the Uniform Standards of Professional Appraisal Practice (USPAP) promulgated by The Appraisal Foundation. However, some states neither require appraisers to be licensed nor regulate licensed appraisers for other than mortgage-connected appraisals; these states also exempt mortgage loan appraisals that are not supervised by lender-regulating federal agencies.

Designated and associate members of the Appraisal Institute agree to uphold the Uniform Standards of Professional Appraisal Practice for the development and reporting of *all* appraisals, and to uphold the Appraisal Institute's Supplemental Standards and its Code of Professional Ethics. Furthermore, the Appraisal Institute imposes its rules and regulations on its members' site-specific *nonvalue* opinions of the utility, the quality, or the nature of identified property aspects or interests. For example, arranging for a nonvalue appraisal fee to be a function of the number of dwelling units estimated to be the highest and best use of a parcel of apartment land is a violation of Appraisal Institute Supplemental Standard 1. As another example, a member engaged by an apartment developer to estimate the internal rate of return that the developer's proposal will yield to limited partnership equity investors (i.e., an estimate of feasibility) for a fee contingent upon successful marketing of the private offering would violate the same supplemental standard. To say such a nonvalue opinion is "not an appraisal" in no way lessens the responsibility imposed by the Appraisal Institute's unambiguous Supplemental Standards Rules.

Some clients refer to written appraisal reports as appraisals; this practice should be discouraged, although it is analogous to the usage in some other nonmedical professions (e.g., a judicial opinion is the written expression of the court's determination).

Appraisers, as distinct from some other professionals, are responsible as individuals for their professional conduct and reporting. Generally, appraisers are not eligible to practice as professional corporations and are not willing to practice in partnerships.

Under narrow circumstances, an appraisal may be completed but never reported in writing, usually because the client associates either no business advantage, or an evidentiary disadvantage, to having a written version of the appraiser's conclusion that has been reported orally. In other cases, presumably, an appraiser is unable or unwilling to prepare a written report.

Most oral appraisal reports, however, are merely advance notice of the chief contents of a written appraisal report soon to be delivered. Indeed, apart from the single-family mortgage appraisal market where the practice is rare, it can be said that many written appraisal reports are preceded by an oral report of the same appraisal opinion. It is neither inaccurate nor improper to refer to the earlier oral report as a preliminary report of the appraisal. By contrast, the phrase *preliminary appraisal* is not a term of art, is nowhere authoritatively defined, and (unless the appraiser reports a precise definition) probably means nothing different from an unreliable appraisal.

The Uniform Standards of Professional Appraisal Practice establish the minimum competency level. Permitted departure from the minimum is restricted. Even then, it requires that the client be aware of and agree to the departure and that precise disclosure be made in any appraisal report of the nature and extent that the Standards Rules have been avoided as well as the import of the departure(s) on the value estimate.

Client Prerogative

Selection of the type of appraisal report to be produced is within the purview of the client, provided, of course, that the report complies with USPAP. The client may instruct that the appraisal report include information extraneous to the valuation. The client may not instruct the appraiser to omit necessary material unless its inclusion is inappropriate legally.

Most clients, for most categories of appraisal most of the time, expect that appraisal opinions will be both developed and reported in accordance with the Uniform Standards. Written appraisal reports of apartment building valuations are often narrative in nature and styled as a typical business report. In other cases, they are lengthy business letters with attachments. The Uniform Standards require that certain aspects of the property and its valuation be included in any written report; a similar list is required for oral reports.

It is not unusual for clients to provide a list of items to be addressed in each apartment property appraisal report, or an order of presentation or even a table of contents to be followed. This practice is an effort to attain a high degree of uniformity. To facilitate the appraisal review procedures of high-volume clients, even greater uniformity of inclusion and reporting order can be attained with a fill-in-the-blanks form on which the appraisal opinion is reported. Mortgage lenders who are active in the secondary mortgage market may require appraisals of two-, three-, or four-family buildings to be reported on a form authorized jointly by Freddie Mac, Fannie Mae, and Ginnie Mae. For larger properties, some clients require, others permit, and yet others eschew forms distributed by Fannie Mae or other organizations. The Federal Housing Administration often specifies apartment property appraisal report forms devised to reveal the exact information that agency must analyze when conforming to precisely identified mortgage title regulations.

One of the large life insurance companies issues a blank document in which appraisers report apartment property appraisals. The document is a combination of forms, formats, and spaces for narrative descriptions that, together with specified attachments, constitutes a form report of sorts exceeding 40 pages.

Some appraisers acquire or devise forms and formats that are integrated for optional use with their word processing software.

Oral Reporting

Oral appraisal reports are more often than not made by telephone to a single person representing the appraiser's client. In this context, the term client does not exclude individuals who make decisions about acquiring, maintaining, or disposing of real estate interests and who work for the same employer as the field appraiser or an affiliated organization. The principal identifications (e.g., property, interest, effective date, value definition), the client's instructions and appraiser's assumptions, the descriptions (e.g., subject property, benchmark transactions), and the reasoning should be communicated.

An oral appraisal report may be given to a group of persons representing the client, including legal or financial advisors, administrators, directors, tenant association boards, family heirs, etc.

Oral appraisal reports are provided to the client's adversary directly, if the appraiser is deposed, or indirectly, if the appraiser is called to testify before a municipal board (e.g., alcoholic beverage control, zoning, rent control, assessment, preservation), an arbitration panel, or a court (with the triers of fact being either commissioners, jurors, or a judge). An appraiser's oral report given in an adversarial forum may include defensive testimony that would not otherwise be reported, such as non-indicative transactions that the appraiser explains are flawed and should be disregarded.

It is often appropriate for the appraiser to present written materials during an in-person oral appraisal report, including summaries of calculations, lists of supporting transactional data, linear exhibits such as a plot plan of the apartment property or floor plans of the units, and photographs with captions. The appraiser should ensure that the papers distributed as aids in making an oral appraisal report are not construed as a written appraisal report; this can be accomplished by editing.

In some cases an oral appraisal report is given after delivery of a written report to which the orally reporting appraiser might refer.

In any case, rules under Standard 2 of USPAP set forth precise minimum requirements for oral appraisal reports. As is the case with written reports, the minimum may be exceeded.

According to USPAP, when an appraisal opinion is not the subject of a written appraisal report, it must be the subject of a detailed memorandum to the appraiser's file. In any case, the appraiser must maintain a file for every appraisal extending for a period of years after the last time it was reported, whether orally, in writing, or both.

Report Organization

Appraisers generally strive, at least initially, to develop each selected appraisal approach independently; as a result, the reporting of the respective approaches, if not on a form, may be in any order that the results of reconciliation and the appraiser's writing style dictate. Successful appraisers rely on the valuation process, while realizing that no one step is invariably more important, or need be processed or reported in any preordained sequence. In fact, some approaches are omitted entirely from time to time.

Usually, however, appraisers find it convenient to identify the real estate, appraised rights, effective date, known intended users of the report and their intended use of the appraisal, limiting conditions, and scope of the data employed, early in the report.

Information about the market in general, as well as a compilation of pertinent transactions (rent, expense, sale, cost, etc.), and about the community and neighborhood tend to be researched simultaneously. What is reported, however, amounts to organized distillations of the more important facts and the appraiser's interpretations of them.

Some appraisers include all the germane transactional data in the section where each respective approach is reported; others group all transactional data in detailed schedules, and introduce only summaries of the benchmark comparables within the respective valuation approach sections of the report. Transaction comparables, when included in appraisal reports, are usually numbered for ease in their identification on location maps and elsewhere. When it is otherwise convenient to do so, consecutive numbering of all the comparables rather than starting each schedule with Comparable 1 is recommended. Consecutive numbering eliminates the possibility for confusion caused by duplicate numbering and it also results in the same number applying to a property that is, for example, both a land sale comparable and a cost comparable, or both a rent comparable and an expense comparable. Some appraisers include photographs as part of the comparable data schedules. Others group them in a separate section.

Often appraisers of apartment properties believe that physical proximity is a more important attribute for rent comparables than for sale comparables or more important for land comparables than for cost and expense comparables. For this reason, they often use separate location maps for each category of comparable data. In other cases, however, an appraiser may include but a single comparable map indicating different comparable categories by color. On maps, the color red seems almost universally reserved to denote the appraised property. When color is not used, the letter "S" is used to identify the location of the subject property.

If a sufficiently expensive grade of paper is used, the appraisal report can be duplicated on both sides of a page. Many appraisers appear to prefer the traditional format of printing and numbering the right-hand pages only. Loose-leaf binding is not popular. At the other extreme, clients are said to remark, perhaps apocryphally, that glued (or sewn) bindings indicate excessive fees. Several semipermanent binding types exist.

Appraiser's Signature

Appraisers (apart from those on the staffs of accounting partnerships) generally sign a letter that transmits their appraisal report to the client. This transmittal letter usually reveals the valuation amount and, for those appraisers who believe signing each report only once is adequate, it will include the appraiser's certification as well. If the transmittal letter includes an appraisal estimate, its language and its inclusion in the table of contents should make clear that the letter is part of the appraisal report and has no validity if detached from it. Without this safeguard, the letter bearing the appraiser's value opinion and signature may meet the Uniform Standards definition of an appraisal report without conforming to the minimum requirements for reporting. The potential difficulty does not arise if the letter per se does conform to all requirements for written appraisal reports or if the appraisal opinion is omitted from the letter. Under USPAP, any communication of an appraiser's value opinion is an appraisal report; it is insufficient to label such a communication "not an appraisal report."

Although USPAP does not require a transmittal letter, there is a requirement that each written appraisal report include a certification. Each individual who signs such a certification thereby signifies

1. A self-proclaimed adequacy to make such an appraisal

2. An undiminished acceptance of the appraisal opinion

3. An uncurtailed professional responsibility for the entire contents of the appraisal report

A nonsigning individual who is acknowledged in the certification as having provided significant professional assistance is not presumed to have responsibility for the report or necessarily to be in agreement with (or even be aware of) the appraisal opinion.

The design of appraisal report covers, the letterhead used, and other pages of a written appraisal report must comply with ethical rules regarding the proprietary nature of trademarks and the public interest and positions regarding promotion and advertising. Otherwise, an appraisal firm is free to adopt stationery that suits the business image it seeks to attain or maintain. The firm's selection of paper stock, print style, and the use or non-use of logos will, over time, identify and partly form the image of the appraiser. An early and continuing decision by the appraiser is whether the image is to suggest a successful business or, alternatively, suggest an office of professionals. A companion decision should be made regarding whether the image is to connote a utilitarian operation or one appealing to a more exclusive niche.

Professionalism

Practitioners in many lines of work provide professional opinions. They include auto mechanics, meteorologists, lawyers, physicians, auditors, securities analysts, economists, and, of course, appraisers. Each category of work faces a general set of challenges to credibility, which each practitioner meets with varying degrees of confidence. In each opinion field, the practitioner should have

1. The intellectual capacity for the work

2. A consistent dedication to the avoidance of bias

3. Reasoning ability gained through education, training, and experience

It is generally acknowledged that, in relation to other fields in which professional opinions are rendered, appraisers achieve a high level of accuracy. Among the reasons is that the relatively small body of knowledge to master allows a higher percentage of appraisers to gain proficiency than would otherwise be the case. The principal reasons, however, are the nature of the work, which is a combination of science and art (the science of quantity—i.e., mathematics—and the skills of induction, deduction, and persuasion), and the detailed way appraisal opinions are communicated.

In the latter context, the elements of a good oral or written appraisal report include the following:

- A good report is clear. It is not capable of being misunderstood. For example, data that appear contradictory should be addressed.

- A good report is precise, not inadvertent.

- A good report is concise, which requires organizing all before reporting any and which in no sense precludes beneficial emphasis by repetition.

- A good report is comprehensive. An appraiser's report is always partial and incomplete relative to everything ascertained and analyzed, but should include enough to meet the expectations of a reasonably impartial client.

- A good report is learned. It demonstrates knowledge of both language usage and appraisal theory.

- A good report's medium is presentable. It has an appropriate appearance, whether the medium is a witness or a document.

Appraisers of competence and integrity should (and do) want to be successful, and it is reasonable to relate success to above-average quality performance. Ideally, a successful appraiser's reconciled value opinions and appraisal reports should be 1) at least equal to the quality of the work of the client's own organization and of professionals in other fields who report to the client, and 2) surpassing the quality of the successful appraiser's competitors. Whether the appraisal reports have a marketing versus a professional cast may reflect the nature of the clients, the competition (either imitative or contrarian), and the personality of the appraiser.

Whereas many of the USPAP requirements are not matters of degree, to the extent that they are, each appraiser is free to exceed the imposed minimum professional standards by, for example, providing more painstaking verifications to improve the accuracy of the data, more applications of the data, and more expansive acknowledgement of instructions and reporting limitations, and of the nature of inspections.

Although it is not necessary to adopt the positions of the late W. Edwards Deming, or his archrival J. M. Juran, or any other quality consultant, certain conclusions about appraisal quality seem reasonable. An appraiser whose opinions and reports are of excellent quality will attract better employees, whose work will require less correction and permit expeditious completion. This will in turn further enhance the reputation of the firm and the security of its fees. It is likely that appraisers who strive for high quality will find that excellence and profitability go hand in hand, whether the office is in a high volume or boutique operation.

Clarity Considerations

It is important that the appraiser's report not be misunderstood. For example, some clients ask that appraisers report the length of marketing time before the effective comparable dates, when the respective interests of the sale comparables and the rent comparables were listed or advertised as available. If the appraiser incorporates that information into the valuation process, it is all well and good. However, if the information is extraneous, the report should clarify that its inclusion is for the use of the client and not integral to the appraisal. Market value definitions all state or imply a controlling condition of adequate market exposure, but that condition, which includes consideration of the nature of the marketing and the sought price, is not just equal to the lapsed time between listing and conveyance. For example, a garden apartment project that has been on the market for two years might suddenly sell as the result of a recent shift in investor confidence. Another garden apartment project might sell for the same reason, although on the market for only a few months. The situation is analogous to (but not the same as) price level shifts dealt with by "time" adjustments. For example, paired sales indicating a 15% market price level drop between two years ago and today do not necessarily instruct the appraiser that the price decline was gradual, nor how much, if any, time adjustment should be applied to a comparable sale occurring six months ago.

Other issues requiring care in reporting include the following:

- Value ambivalence (e.g., sensitivity analyses, confidence intervals).

- Confusion between highest and best use of the real estate and the business operation of that use. (For example, the highest and best use is as a rental apartment building, but is it for singles or elderly, furnished or unfurnished, and so forth?)

- The discard of an inconveniently priced comparable.

- The various relationships between capitalization and discount rates on one hand, and value on the other. (For example, processing income with a high rate produces a low value. But were the amount of income greater, either the rate would be higher or the value would be higher—unless the higher income resulted from the more risky operation of the property, in which case the value might be the same if the more risky operation could be replaced, or less if it could not.)

Finally, the appraisal report should include jargon if it facilitates understanding, but for no other reason. Similarly, adjectives are often helpful, too many adjectives less so. A report stating that the monthly rent is at the rate of "$1.15 per square foot" might be improved if it read "per net square foot," but would be rendered either redundant or inaccurate (as well as cumbersome) if it read "per net occupiable square foot."

Reviewing

Clients and others closely inspect the fairly detailed reports prepared by appraisers. The advice provided to clients by other professionals is usually more terse. As with other fields, the appraiser's work is technical, but the style of report permits the appraiser's conclusions, the nature of the data justifying the conclusions, and at least the general methodology to be grasped by most educated adults. Almost everyone who has a reason to hear or read an appraisal report is able to make a business judgment in its regard. Citizen boards of municipalities and counties, and even open-minded citizens observing hearings conducted by such boards are, or are not, persuaded to an appraiser's point of view. Petit jurors, of course, are required to base awards on the oral (and sometimes written) reports of appraisers. In other law cases, judges may quote or paraphrase one or more appraisal reports when explaining their decisions, as do commissioners, masters, or examiners in other forums.

It is necessary that accountants preparing income tax returns, and Internal Revenue Service agents reviewing the returns, comprehend the appraisal reports that accompany them. It is generally thought to be improper for a tax lawyer to accept appraisal advice on behalf of the client unless the lawyer has determined that the advice is reasonable.

Lawyers in many specialties read and listen to appraisal reports. Some, of course, are litigators defending or prosecuting criminals, bringing or resisting civil suits for damages or claims, seeking zoning or assessment relief, and so forth. Other lawyers are real estate counselors, contract negotiators, transaction representatives, business agents, corporate directors, and organizational administrators and managers. In all of those pursuits, the lawyers' judgment is sought regarding the business sufficiency as well as the legal sufficiency of appraisal reports. Other businesspeople who are not lawyers and who occupy board rooms, executive suites, and public positions also believe they understand the appraisal reports upon which they act.

Review Appraisers

In contrast to the many who make business judgments regarding the appraisal reports they examine, there are others with the unique task of making professional appraisal judgments of the adequacy of the written appraisal reports they review. Those in their midst who have so qualified (i.e., those who have earned the professional respect of field appraisers and have assumed the professional obligations of review appraisers) are presumed to carry out their work impartially and to be experts in the valuation process. Review appraisers are found on the staffs of organizations that contract for a high volume of appraisal reports, particularly government bureaus and mortgage lenders. Smaller organizations in government or commerce from time to time contract for review appraiser services to manage an unusual volume or to obtain a property type specialist.

A staff review appraiser may have an assistant peruse an appraisal report in a nontechnical sense for such matters as

1. Determining whether any contract-required inclusions were omitted by the field appraiser

2. Completing a form-summary or digest of the field appraiser's report

3. Ascertaining which, if any, arithmetic errors were reported by the field appraiser.

Requests and suggestions to the field appraiser by an assistant to the reviewer generally regard factual and, hence, noncontroversial corrections.

In contrast, the review appraiser will make sufficiency judgments regarding the following:

1. The quantity and quality of the data

2. The procedures used to process it

3. The adequacy of experts upon whom the field appraiser has relied

4. The extent to which the field appraiser has limited the value opinion

5. The underlying theory and reasoning

The Review Appraiser's Alternatives

If all goes well, a review appraiser will determine that a field appraiser's report is not technically deficient in a major way and can be passed on to the negotiator, manager, decision maker, or whoever will make or recommend the business decision involved. In other cases, however, the review appraiser will conclude that the field appraiser's information is inadequate, the processing illogical, the reasoning flawed by internal conflict, or the conclusion unsubstantiated.

Depending upon the circumstances, or perhaps the policies of the organization, the field appraiser might be asked to reconsider one or more aspects. For example, the review appraiser asks the field appraiser to factor in some newly ascertained comparable data or discuss a differing interpretation of a provision in a ground lease. In another case, the review appraiser decides that the field appraiser's report supports a range of value in which a pending transaction lies, although it is at a different amount than the point value certified to by the field appraiser. In yet another case, the review appraiser decides that the field appraiser has expressed an opinion that conflicts with the opinions of others—say, on the recent market trend, the merit of the subject location, or the appropriate vacancy or capitalization rate—and but for this opinion, the value conclusion would have been different. The field appraiser could be asked to report that different amount as a possible alternative justification for the business at hand. A condemnor might use that technique to support a just compensation court deposit filed coincidentally with the declaration of taking, or toward a negotiated settlement. In either case, the field appraiser's opinion, although different from the deposit or the offer, is preserved should trial testimony be necessary.

In none of these examples has the review appraiser certified to an opinion of value. Another alternative, of course, is for the erstwhile review appraiser, if eligible under state law, to conduct an appraisal and take responsibility for an estimate of value.

One remaining alternative is open to a review appraiser: to request a valuation and report from an appraiser who has had no previous involvement in the matter.

Appraiser Impartiality

The review function as conducted by review appraisers is similar to and alleviated by a successful quality control function in the field appraiser's office. Whether the review is internal or external (client-initiated), that reviewing individual, whether staff or contract, should not look for, much less insist upon, a direction in value that favors the cause of the client. Within reason, a field appraiser is not surprised or offended by a client's lack of impartiality. Bias on the part of a review appraiser, however, is conduct contrary to the review appraiser's certification.

Test of Reasonableness

Other than when they are merely determining compliance with the rules of engagement, review appraisers are primarily judging against a test of reasonableness in which they pose and answer such questions as the following:

- In the absence of a cost approach, what amount of building contribution is implied by the difference between the reported land value and total value? Is it a reasonable amount in light of the building and neighborhood descriptions?

- In the absence of a capitalization procedure, what overall capitalization rate is implied by the quotient of dividing the appraiser's net income stabilization (or last year's net income) by the conclusion? Is it a reasonable rate in view of the market data that the field appraiser reported?

- Were the data processed using a reasonable number of units of comparison? For example, are the expenses and rents reasonable on a per-room or on a gross-square-foot basis?

- Is the expense ratio consistent with the reported data?

- Is the debt coverage ratio reasonable?

- Are the selected elements of comparison logical?

- If an adjustment grid is reported, is the magnitude of adjustment in each case reasonable in view of the respective property descriptions?

- Were apparent data conflicts reasonably reconciled?

The Field Appraiser's Obligations

A review appraiser expects the field appraiser to describe a reasonable amount of market data selected because of physical, functional, locational, and chronological similarity, to analyze the data in accordance with land economics principles and the valuation process, and to report the conclusions in a literate way using a reasonable (often client-specified) format.

It should be clear to the review appraiser whether the hypothetical seller is to receive all cash equal to the appraised value and, if not, the terms of any seller-arranged financing. If the appraisal is conducted in a dislocated market where sales are scarce, the field appraiser's perspective of value should be clear. Is the value estimate reported equal to the amount a typical willing seller, free of duress, would accept or to the lower amount, which is all a typical willing purchaser, free of duress, will pay? Is the field appraiser adequately distinguishing between cost (ordinarily the upper limit of value) and cost approach (ordinarily an indication of value)? Does the field appraiser adequately distinguish among the contract date, conveyance date, and recording date, as well as among the effective date, analysis date, and reporting date?

Summary and Conclusion

After all other steps in developing an appraisal opinion have been taken, the ultimate opinion is then reached through the process of reconciliation, which is meant to ensure that no inconsistency revealed by the appraisal process has not been confronted. Usually, the various types of transactional information culminate in unequal preliminary conclusions from valuation approaches. Whereas perfect analysis applied to complete data would theoretically produce equal results from each appraisal approach, unequal preliminary conclusions are to be expected. It is unnecessary, and not attempted, to research all of the information that might be analyzed. The appraiser's mental powers are imperfect, and the transaction amounts are likely to reflect subjective considerations such as differing negotiating skills, levels of duress, knowledge, and emotion. The perspective of appraisers is the price for which the property will sell rather than the price for which it ought to sell. The value is the amount the market thinks it is, even though a computer, for example, processing unlimited data with dispassionate calculations might conclude a lesser or greater sum.

The notion of analytical consistency allows for differing results from the approaches employed, differing points of view, and even differing opinions. An appraiser does not reconcile differences away but rather confronts them and explains why they occur. In developing the appraisal, this explanation of apparent but justified inconsistencies is internal. In reporting the appraisal, the reconciliation and the appraiser's ultimate conclusion of value, in oral or written text, is designed to convince the user or those who contemplate some action or decision related to the appraiser's advice. In an effort to be convincing, the appraiser has various philosophical and psychological alternatives available, more than one of which can be reported in the reconciliation section.

The appraisal methods and techniques are almost entirely determined by the appraiser; the appraisal report order and presentation are to a large extent determined by the client. In other words, the opinion is entirely that of the appraiser whereas the presentation of the opinion is influenced by the client. In general, the client may not delete items the appraiser wants reported (or is professionally required to report), but may request inclusion of other items so long as no reader of the report would be misled.

Because appraisers sometimes make mistakes in their work, an internal quality control process is recommended. A trusted colleague can critique the appraisal and appraisal report before the report is released to the client.

In some instances, appraisers abuse their professional responsibilities. The most common are the actions of the obsequious appraisers who mistakenly associate success in the appraisal business with servile adoption of their clients' positions. When the result is appraisal opinions that depart from market value, of course, the practice is inherently inconsistent with the valuation process. A review of the work product by an impartial appraisal expert will generally reveal this.

For the most part, however, field appraisers pursue their work diligently, patiently, and intelligently, demonstrating competence and exercising integrity. Usually, their appraisal reports are clear and convincing distillations of what they have researched and why they have formed their opinions. Generally, review appraisers are reasonably satisfied with the field appraisal reports they review and reasonably convinced of the opinions contained in them.

Bibliography

Textbooks and Monographs

Appraisal Institute. *The Appraisal of Real Estate,* 11th ed. Chicago: Appraisal Institute, 1996.

_____ . *Appraising Residential Properties,* 2d ed. Chicago: Appraisal Institute, 1994.

_____ . *Highest and Best Use and Market Analysis,* course manual. Chicago: Appraisal Institute, 1992.

Everett, E. Roger, and William N. Kinnard. *A Guide to Appraising Apartments.* Chicago: Society of Real Estate Appraisers, 1979.

Gunn, Eleanor, and John Simpson. *Cooperative Apartment Appraisal.* Chicago: Appraisal Institute, 1997.

Horowitz, Carl E. *The New Garden Apartment: Current Market Realities of an American Housing Form.* Rutgers, N.J.: Center for Urban Policy Research, Rutgers University, 1983.

O'Connell, Daniel J. *The Appraisal of Apartment Buildings.* New York: John Wiley & Sons, 1989.

Paul, Samuel. *Apartments: Their Design and Development.* New York: Reinhold Publishing, 1967.

Data Sources

Appraisal Institute. *Annual Economic Forecast 1997*. Chicago: Appraisal Institute, 1997.

Institute of Real Estate Management. *Conventional Apartments: Income/Expense Analysis.* Chicago: Institute of Real Estate Management, 1997. Published annually.

Multifamily Housing Institute, an affiliate of the Urban Land Institute, maintains an on-line database, Apt*Data,* which provides subscribing members with information on the performance of multifamily properties and mortgage loans.

Urban Land Institute in association with the National Apartment Association. *Dollars and Cents of Multifamily Housing 1997—A Survey of Income and Expenses in Rental Apartment Communities.* Washington, D.C.: Urban Land Institute, 1997.

Articles

Crocker, Douglas II, and Matthew B. Slepin. "Multifamily Development Meets the Information Revolution." *Urban Land* (April 1997): 68-71.

Goodman, Jack. "A Look at Consolidation in the Apartment Industry." *Urban Land* (November 1997): 35-37, 76.